cupcakes, cookies & pie, oh, my!

cupcakes, cookies & pie, oh, my!

karen tack & alan richardson

Houghton Mifflin Harcourt

Boston   New York   2012

12 Feb 29
B+T
17.95 (1257

Thank you to Larry, Chris, Erik, Liam, Bunny, and Lucky for keeping our feet on the ground. And a special thanks to our agent, Martha Kaplan, our editor, Rux Martin, production editor Rebecca Springer, marketing manager Katrina Kruse, and designer Elizabeth Van Itallie for your hard work and terrific spirit. You are cupcakers extraordinaire.

Copyright © 2012 by Karen Tack and Alan Richardson

Visit our website: www.hmhbooks.com.
For printable versions of the templates in this book, go to www.hmhbooks.com/cupcakes.

Library of Congress Cataloging-in-Publication Data
Tack, Karen.
Cupcakes, cookies, and pie, oh, my! / Karen Tack and Alan Richardson.
    p. cm.
Includes index.
ISBN 978-0-547-66242-8
1. Cupcakes. 2. Cookies. 3. Pies. 4. Cookbooks.
    I. Richardson, Alan, date. II. Title.
TX771.T315 2012
641.8'653—c23   2011036974

Book design by Elizabeth Van Itallie

Printed in the United States of America
DOW 10 9 8 7 6 5 4 3 2 1

Happy Decorating!

To all the folks who never pass a bakeshop, a candy store, or a cookie aisle without feeling the urge to go in, to anyone who sees treasure in putting a smile on someone's face, and to everyone clever enough to realize that the kitchen is the very best place to play, this book's for you.

Karen Tack   Alan Richardson

CONTENTS

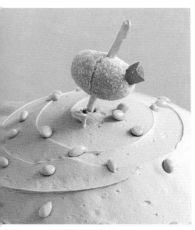

sandwich cookie

cupcake

pig + porcupine = **PORK-UPINE**

we're going hog wild!

In **Hello, Cupcake!** and **What's New, Cupcake?** we showed you how to use candy and snacks to turn cupcakes into clever and unexpected treats. But why stop at cupcakes when cookies, cakes, brownies, rice cereal treats, and pies offer so many possibilities?

We've developed a whole new set of easier-than-ever techniques, too, so you can make even more dramatic creations. We'll show you how to create glossy patterned surfaces with melted frosting, paint with brilliant "egg wash," and shape candy "clay" into everything from clothes for cookie dolls to peacock feathers or even a Chinese dragon.

What are you waiting for? With all of these new treats and techniques, we think your family and friends are going to say, "Cupcakes, cookies, and pie—

oh, my!

build a pet

Sometimes an ant is just an ant. But when it has big floppy ears, a tail, and a long trunk, it's an eleph-ant. Creating a pet is a fun way to discover new candies and snacks for decorating. The animals on the following pages are based on other projects in the book. For example, our eleph-ant is three red Emotipops (page 138) decorated with spice drops for the ears, trunk, and tail, with licorice pastels for the legs. The pork-upine (page 8) is a variation on Pig in a Blanket (page 31), with spines made from pink licorice. And the Zebra-doodle on page 13 is a sheep (page 58) with a zebra pattern (for the technique, see our high-heel shoes, page 115). To get started making your own pets, choose a base for the body: a cupcake, cookie, or cake. Next, make critter parts from soft candy, hard candy, and snacks, mixing and matching to create crazy new creatures. Then pick a name for the pet and find it a good home in need of a smile.

Before you know it, you'll have all the skills you need to tackle your favorite decorating projects.

pound cake

elephant + ant = **ELEPH-ANT**

monkey + crocodile = **MONKEY-DILE**

cookie

pound
cake

cock + fish = **COCK-A-FISH**

rice cereal
treat

snail + pelican = **SNAIL-ICAN**

cookie or
cupcake

swan + turtle = **SWAN-URTLE**

pretzel

cupcake

pound cake

sandwich
cookie

zebra + poodle = **ZEBRA-DOODLE**

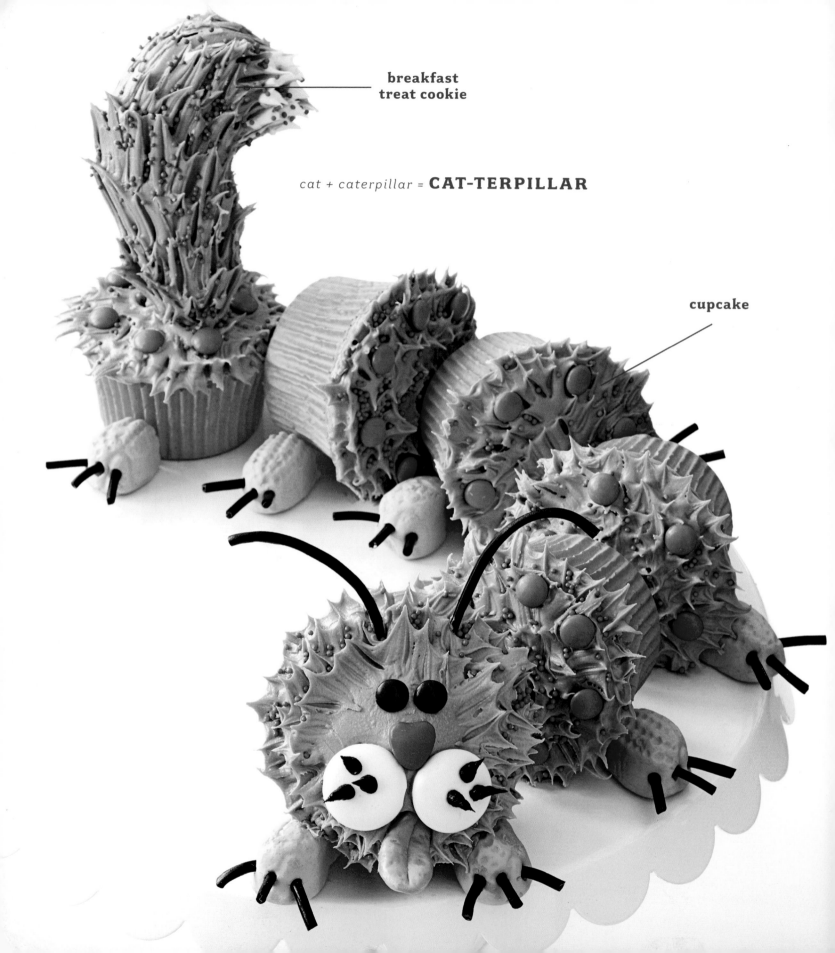

breakfast treat cookie

cat + caterpillar = **CAT-TERPILLAR**

cupcake

hard candy parts

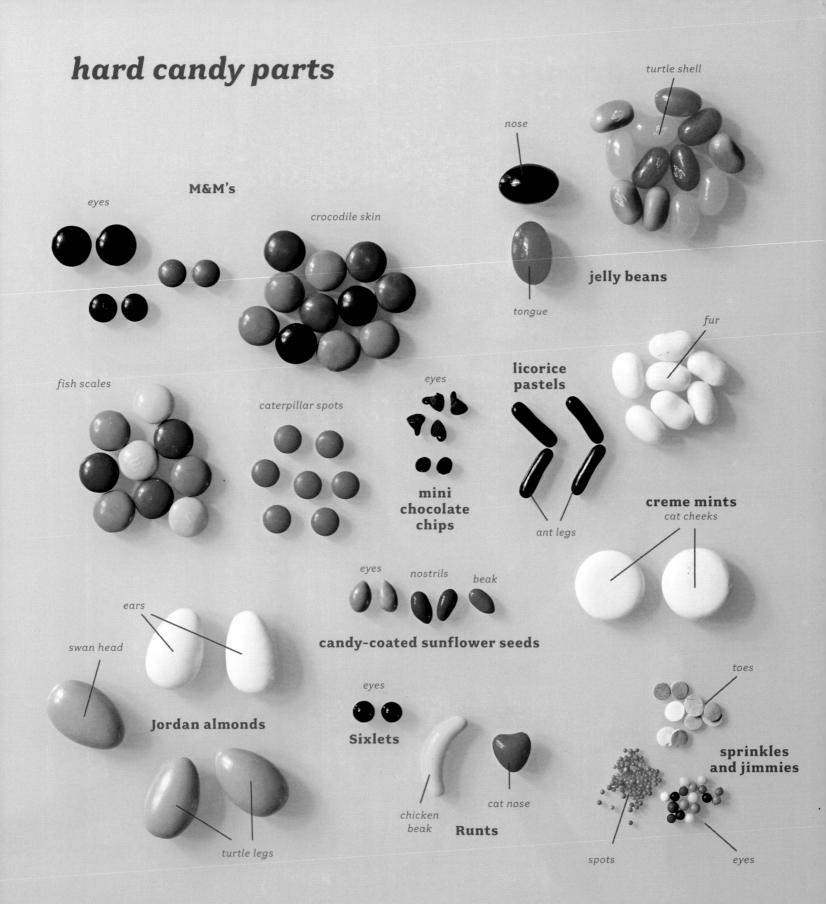

eyes

M&M's

crocodile skin

nose

turtle shell

jelly beans

tongue

fish scales

caterpillar spots

eyes

licorice pastels

fur

mini chocolate chips

ant legs

creme mints
cat cheeks

eyes

nostrils

beak

candy-coated sunflower seeds

ears

swan head

Jordan almonds

toes

eyes

Sixlets

sprinkles and jimmies

chicken beak

cat nose

Runts

turtle legs

spots

eyes

soft candy parts

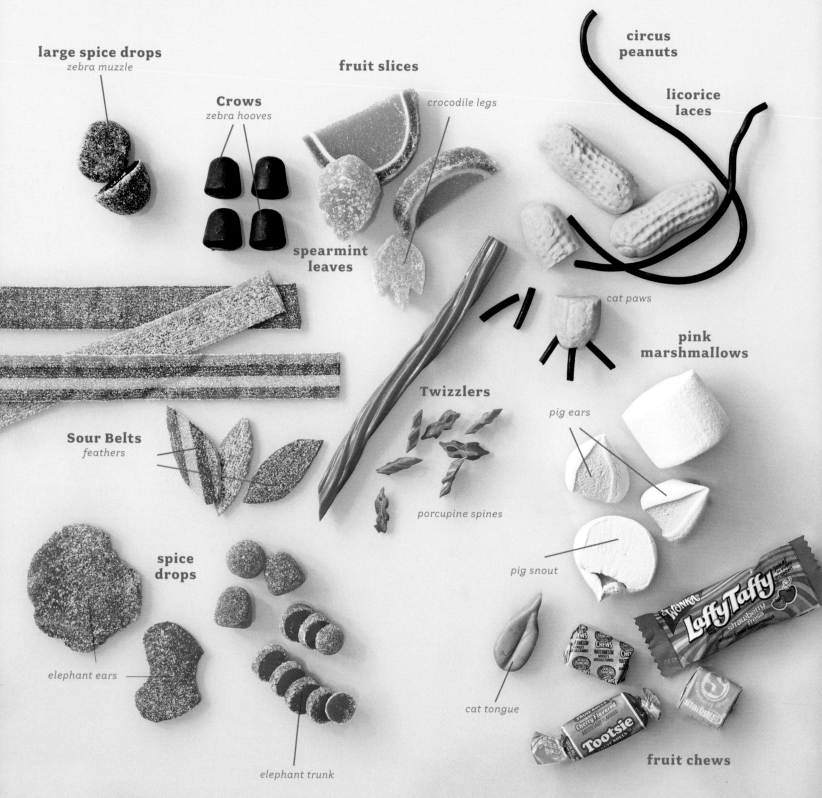

large spice drops
zebra muzzle

Crows
zebra hooves

fruit slices
crocodile legs

circus peanuts

licorice laces
cat paws

spearmint leaves

Sour Belts
feathers

Twizzlers

porcupine spines

pink marshmallows
pig ears

pig snout

spice drops

elephant ears

elephant trunk

cat tongue

fruit chews

Laffy Taffy strawberry fresa

CHEWS WATERMELON

CHEWS

Cherry Flavored Tootsie FRUIT ROLLS

Starburst

snack parts

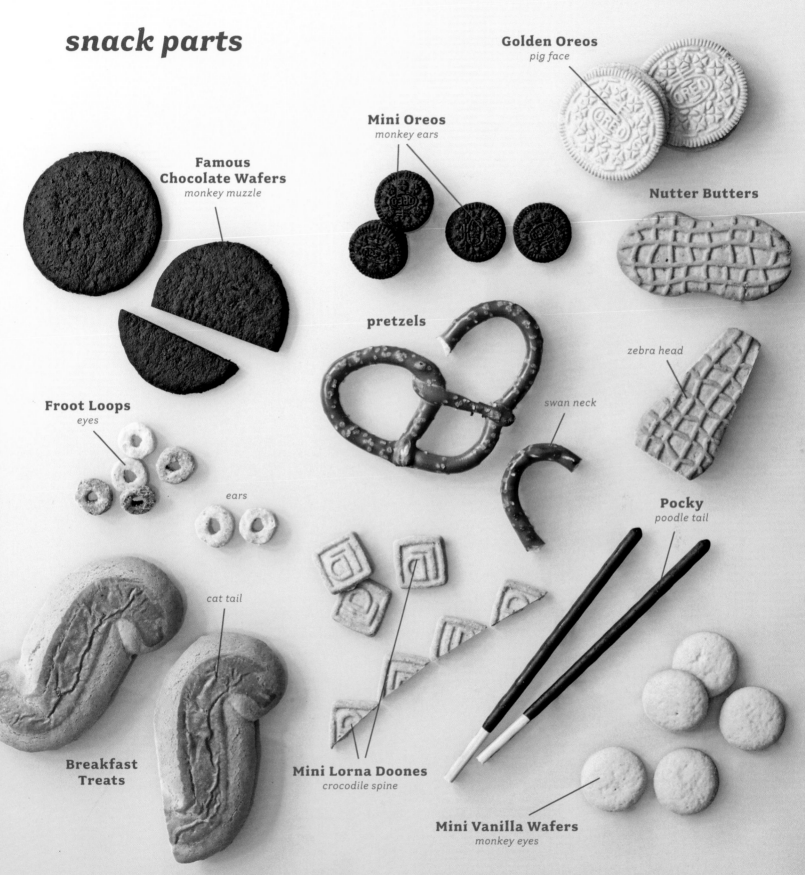

Golden Oreos
pig face

Mini Oreos
monkey ears

Famous Chocolate Wafers
monkey muzzle

Nutter Butters

pretzels

zebra head

swan neck

Froot Loops
eyes

ears

Pocky
poodle tail

Breakfast Treats

cat tail

Mini Lorna Doones
crocodile spine

Mini Vanilla Wafers
monkey eyes

make 'em laugh

What did the cookie say to the pie when the spatula walked in? That puts the icing on the cake! These confections will leave them laughing and begging for more. Why settle for pie when you can have a Pie in the Face?

PIE IN THE FACE

MAKES 12 PIES

Who knew a mustache and glasses could make pie so much fun? A topper made from cookie dough is the easiest way to give pie a fresh face.

- **1 recipe Quick Chocolate Cookie Dough (page 227)**
- **½ cup canned vanilla frosting**
- **1½ cups canned dark chocolate frosting**
- **6 marshmallows**
- **12 mini marshmallows**
- **1 can (1.5 ounces) red decorating spray (Betty Crocker)**
- **24 brown candy-coated chocolates (M&M's)**
- **4 cups store-bought vanilla pudding, prepared according to package directions**
  Red food coloring
- **12 mini graham cracker crusts (Keebler Ready Crust)**

1 Cut out and bake the cookie dough as directed on page 227, using the face template below to make 12 cookies.

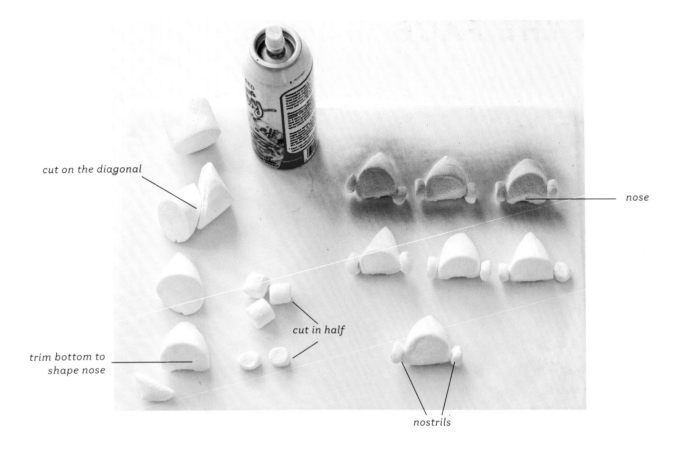

cut on the diagonal

nose

cut in half

trim bottom to shape nose

nostrils

2 Spoon the vanilla and the dark chocolate frostings into separate ziplock bags. Press out the excess air and seal the bags. For the noses, cut each large marshmallow in half on the diagonal. Trim the flat end of each triangle to shape the bottom of the nose (see above). For the nostrils, cut the mini marshmallows in half crosswise. Snip a small (⅛-inch) corner from the bag with the vanilla frosting. Pipe a dot of frosting on the cut sides of the mini marshmallows. Attach 1 mini marshmallow to each side of the large marshmallow noses, as shown. Place the noses on a sheet of waxed paper. Spray with the red decorating spray to coat lightly.

3 For the glasses, microwave the bag of vanilla frosting for no more than 3 seconds to soften. Pipe the white lens area on the face cookies with the softened vanilla frosting. Add the chocolate candies for the pupils. Snip a small (⅛-inch) corner from the bag with the chocolate frosting. Pipe the eyebrows and mustaches on the face cookies with the chocolate frosting. Pipe a dot of chocolate frosting and attach the noses.

4 Tint the vanilla pudding light pink with the red food coloring. Divide the pudding among the mini graham cracker crusts. Top with the face cookies.

PIE IN THE SKY

MAKES 6 SUNNY FACES

Your cookie cutters are the secret to more cookie pie ideas. Try using a sun-shaped cutter and cut out a hole in the center to let lemon filling shine through.

½ **recipe Quick Sugar Cookie Dough (page 226)**
¼ **cup canned vanilla frosting**
    Yellow food coloring
3 **tablespoons light corn syrup (Karo)**
½ **cup orange decorating sugar (Cake Mate)**
2 **cups store-bought lemon pudding, prepared according to package directions**
6 **mini graham cracker crusts (Keebler Ready Crust)**
¼ **cup semisweet chocolate chips**

1 Cut and bake the cookie dough as directed on page 226, using a 5-inch sun cookie cutter (see Sources). Remove the center area with a 2¼-inch round cookie cutter or small knife before baking.

2 Tint the vanilla frosting yellow with the food coloring. Spoon the frosting into a ziplock bag, press out the excess air, and seal the bag.

3 Place the corn syrup in a small bowl. Microwave the corn syrup until bubbly, 5 to 7 seconds. Working on 1 cookie at a time, brush a thin layer of corn syrup on top of the cookie to cover completely. Sprinkle the top of the cookie with the orange sugar to coat. Repeat with the remaining cookies and sugar. Reheat the corn syrup in the microwave for about 5 seconds if it becomes too thick to brush.

4 Snip a small (⅛-inch) corner from the bag with the frosting. Pipe small zigzag lines of frosting on the sugared cookies to make the sunrays. Repeat with all of the cookies; set aside.

5 Spoon the lemon pudding into the mini graham cracker crusts.

6 Place the chocolate chips in a ziplock bag; do not seal the bag. Microwave for 10 seconds to soften. Massage the chips in the bag, return to the microwave, and repeat the process until the chocolate is smooth, about 30 seconds. Press out the excess air and seal the bag. Snip a very small (1/16-inch) corner from the bag and pipe the faces on the lemon pudding. Arrange the sun cookies on the pies just before serving.

NACHO NORMAL CHEESECAKE

MAKES 1 CHEESECAKE; ABOUT 10 SERVINGS

And these are definitely not your normal nachos either! Made from piecrust sprinkled with sugar, they sit atop a delicious lemon cheesecake with a sour cream frosting. Toss on some strawberry-jam salsa and top with candy olives for the funniest nacho night ever. Olé!

CHEESECAKE
Nonstick cooking spray
2 **packages (8 ounces each) cream cheese, at room temperature**
⅔ **cup plus ¼ cup sugar**
1 **teaspoon lemon zest**
2 **tablespoons lemon juice**
1 **teaspoon vanilla extract**
3 **large eggs**
Yellow and red food coloring
½ **cup sour cream**

NACHO CHIPS
1 **roll refrigerated pie dough (Pillsbury)**
All-purpose flour
1 **tablespoon milk**
2 **tablespoons sugar**

GARNISHES AND SALSA
8 **red Swedish fish**
1 **cup low-sugar strawberry preserves (Smucker's)**
3 **green licorice twists (Kenny's Green Apple Juicy Twists)**
6 **black licorice dots (Crows)**
3 **tablespoons sour cream**
Yellow and red food coloring
3 **tablespoons chocolate-covered raisins (Raisinets)**

1 **CHEESECAKE:** Preheat the oven to 350°F. Spray a 9-inch clear pie plate with nonstick cooking spray. Beat the cream cheese in a large bowl with an electric mixer on medium speed until smooth. Add the ⅔ cup sugar, lemon zest, lemon juice, and vanilla and beat well. Add the eggs, one at a time, beating well after each addition until smooth. Tint the batter orange with the yellow and red food coloring and stir until evenly blended.

2 Pour the batter into the pie plate. Bake the cheesecake until puffed and almost set, 25 to 30 minutes.

3 Stir together the sour cream and the remaining ¼ cup sugar in a small bowl. Gently spread the sour cream mixture over the hot cheesecake, almost to the edge. Return to the oven and bake for 5 minutes longer. Transfer the cheesecake to a wire rack and cool to room temperature. Refrigerate until set, at least 2 hours.

4 **NACHO CHIPS:** Preheat the oven to 400°F. Line two cookie sheets with parchment paper. Unroll the pie dough onto a lightly floured work surface and roll it out to flatten slightly. Brush the top of the dough with the milk and sprinkle with the sugar. With a pastry wheel or knife, cut the dough into 2½-inch-wide strips. Cut each strip into as many 2½-inch triangles as possible. Transfer the triangles to the cookie sheets, about 1 inch apart. Bake in batches until the triangles are lightly golden, 6 to 8 minutes. Transfer to a wire rack and cool completely.

5 **GARNISHES AND SALSA:** For the tomatoes, cut the Swedish fish into ½-inch pieces and toss in 2 tablespoons of the strawberry jam to coat. For the chiles, cut the green licorice on the diagonal into ¼-inch slices. For the olives, cut the black licorice dots into ¼-inch-thick rounds. Use a pastry tip or straw to remove a circle from the center of each round. For the melted cheese, tint the sour cream orange with the yellow and red food coloring. Spoon the sour cream into a ziplock bag. Press out the excess air and seal. For the salsa, add some of the green twists and Swedish fish to the remaining strawberry jam and set aside.

6 To assemble, press some of the nacho chips into the top of the cheesecake. Add the chocolate-covered raisins, licorice dot rounds, the remaining green twists, and the remaining jam-coated Swedish fish pieces to the top. Snip a small (⅛-inch) corner from the bag with the orange-tinted sour cream and pipe a few puddles on top for the cheese.

7 Serve with the salsa and the remaining chips.

olé!

DESSERT FOR BREAKFAST

NO-BAKE • MAKES 8 BREAKFASTS FOR DESSERT

Our favorite meal of the day? Dessert! Even better if it's disguised as breakfast. And you'll want more jam, please, especially if it's fruit-filled gelatin served with slices of pound cake toast and whipped topping shaped to look like sticks of butter.

JARS OF JAM
4 cups white cranberry juice (Ocean Spray) or white grape juice
3 envelopes (0.25 ounce each) unflavored gelatin (Knox)
½ cup sugar
4 cups drained canned or frozen fruit: sliced peaches, pears, mandarin oranges, apricots, and/or strawberries (thaw frozen fruit completely)
Mason jars with lids or other clear containers: two 1-quart, four 2-cup, or eight 1-cup jars
Red food coloring (if making strawberry jam)

BUTTER
1 container (8 ounces) frozen whipped topping (Cool Whip), thawed
Yellow food coloring

TOAST
1 bakery pound cake (Entenmann's or store brand)

1 **JARS OF JAM:** Place 1 cup of the juice in a large bowl. Sprinkle the gelatin over the juice and let stand for about 5 minutes.

2 Heat the remaining 3 cups juice with the sugar in a medium saucepan over medium heat until it just comes to a simmer. Stir until the sugar is dissolved. Pour the hot juice over the gelatin mixture and stir until the gelatin is dissolved. Let the mixture cool slightly.

3 Divide the fruit among the containers: 2 cups in the 1-quart containers, 1 cup in the 2-cup containers, or ½ cup in the 1-cup containers. Pour the gelatin mixture over the fruit to cover (if using strawberries, add a few drops of red food coloring to the gelatin before covering the fruit). Place the lids on the jars and refrigerate until set, about 3 hours.

4 **BUTTER:** Line two mini (3-by-5-inch) loaf pans with waxed paper.

5 Tint the whipped topping pale yellow with the food coloring. Spoon the whipped topping into the pans and smooth (see photo). Freeze until the whipped topping is firm, about 2 hours.

6 Preheat the broiler. Remove the paper liner from the pound cake if necessary. Cut a lengthwise ½-inch notch horizontally into each side of the pound cake about 1 inch down from the top to resemble the crown of a bread loaf. Trim the ends of the pound cake even. Use a serrated knife to cut the cake into eight ¾-inch-thick slices.

7 Place the cake slices close together on a cookie sheet. Toast the cake under the broiler until golden brown; watch carefully. Turn the cake slices over and return to the broiler until golden brown.

8 Cut the frozen whipped topping lengthwise to make 2 sticks of butter. Serve with the toasted cake and jars of jam.

PIGS IN A BLANKET

MAKES ABOUT 20 SERVINGS

These little piggies went "Wee, wee, wee!" all the way to bed. Red and white spice drops rolled into a thin "fabric" are cut into squares and "stitched" to make the blanket. The ears and snouts are made from pink marshmallows, but white marshmallows would be just as sweet.

¾ cup granulated sugar

18 each white and red spice drops

½ cup red decorating sugar (Cake Mate)

2 pink fruit chews (Jolly Rancher, Laffy Taffy)

30 pink or white marshmallows (Kraft Jet-Puffed)

1 can (16 ounces) plus 1 cup vanilla frosting

½ cup dark chocolate frosting
  Red food coloring

1 recipe Perfect Cake Mix (page 224), made with yellow cake,
  divided to make an 8-inch round layer and 11 cupcakes baked in white paper liners

16 brown mini candy-coated chocolates (M&M's Minis)

1 For the blanket, sprinkle the work surface with some of the granulated sugar (reserving ¼ cup). Press 3 white spice drops together and roll out to a 1¾-by-3¼-inch rectangle, adding more sugar if necessary to prevent sticking. Repeat with the remaining white spice drops, then with the red spice drops, rolling them out on the red decorating sugar (see photo). Cut out two 1½-inch squares from each flattened candy rectangle with a 1½-inch square cookie cutter or a small knife and a ruler (do not get sugar on the cut edges; they should remain sticky for assembly).

2 Make a 9-inch square by arranging 6 rows of 6 alternating color spice-drop squares, side by side, and pressing the edges firmly together to adhere. Use the rolling pin to flatten and secure if needed. Cover the blanket with plastic wrap to prevent drying.

3 For the tongues, cut each pink fruit chew into 5 small pieces. Flatten each piece into a small teardrop shape. Press a knife lengthwise on each fruit chew to create a crease, then pinch the small end (see photo).

4 Place the reserved ¼ cup granulated sugar in a small bowl. For the ears, cut 10 marshmallows in half on the diagonal, allowing the pieces to fall into the sugar. Shake the bowl and press the cut sides of the marshmallows into the sugar to coat (see photo). For the snouts, cut a ¾-inch-thick slice crosswise from one flat end of 10 marshmallows, reserving the smaller pieces to use under the blanket. For the mouth, using the larger pieces, cut a slit ¼ inch down from the untrimmed flat side with scissors. Pull open the slit, add the fruit chew tongue, and tuck the marshmallow in above the tongue to shape the snout. Repeat with the remaining snout pieces. For the tail, cut a ¼-inch slice from one long side of a marshmallow. To make the legs and bodies, cut the remaining marshmallows in half lengthwise (see photo).

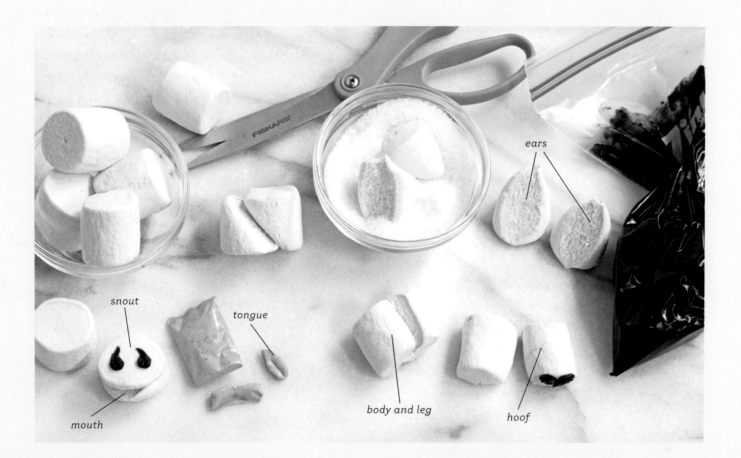

ears

snout

tongue

body and leg

hoof

mouth

5 Spoon ¼ cup of the vanilla frosting and all of the chocolate frosting into separate ziplock bags. Press out the excess air and seal the bags. Tint 1 cup of the remaining vanilla frosting light pink with the red food coloring.

6 Trim the top of the round cake level. Place the cake, cut side down, on a serving platter (the bottom side is flatter). Spread the top and sides of the cake with the remaining vanilla frosting and smooth. Arrange the marshmallow scraps and all but 10 of the halved marshmallow pieces, cut side down, over the top of the cake as the bodies. Place the spice-drop blanket on top of the cake, gently pressing the blanket to conform to the marshmallow pieces. Fold the corners back so the blanket doesn't get coated with the frosting from the side of the cake.

7 Spread the tops of the cupcakes with the pink frosting and smooth. For the ears, arrange 2 sugared marshmallows along the top edge of 10 of the cupcakes, pointed ends up. Position the snout marshmallows on the lower third of these 10 cupcakes. Add the brown candies for the eyes on 8 of these cupcakes. Add the marshmallow tail at one side of the remaining cupcake. Arrange the cupcakes around the outside edge of the cake.

8 Snip a small (⅛-inch) corner from the bags with the vanilla and chocolate frostings. Pipe the closed eyes on 2 of the cupcakes and nostrils on all the pigs except the tail using the chocolate frosting (see photo). Pipe 3 dots of vanilla frosting for the stitching at each corner where the spice drops meet on the blanket. Pipe the hooves on the legs using the chocolate frosting and position the legs on the tail cupcake and next to several other cupcakes. Tuck the piggies under the spice-drop blanket and serve.

FISHWICH

MAKES 1 FISH SANDWICH; ABOUT 36 SERVINGS

What kind of fish do you prefer: haddock, cod, or cake? This fishwich is actually a triple-layer cake: a round layer, a square layer, and on top, a cake that has been baked in a bowl. A coating of toasted cake crumbs gives the middle layer a look that's straight out of the fryer basket.

Nonstick cooking spray
2 recipes Perfect Cake Mix (page 224), made with yellow cake
½ cup sugar
15 candy spearmint leaves (Farley's)
16 orange circus peanuts
2 cans (16 ounces each) vanilla frosting
Yellow food coloring
1½ teaspoons unsweetened cocoa powder
2 tablespoons yellow candy-coated chocolate-covered sunflower seeds (Sunny Seed Drops)
2 large green spice drops
1 large red spice drop
1 thin honey wheat stick (Pringles)
Small plastic cups
2 yellow candy fruit slices

1 Preheat the oven to 350°F. Line an 8-inch round and an 8-inch square cake pan with waxed paper. Spray with nonstick cooking spray. Spray a 1½-quart oven-safe glass bowl with nonstick cooking spray.

2 Pour 2½ cups of the yellow cake batter into the square pan and 2½ cups into the round pan and smooth. Pour the remaining batter into the glass bowl and smooth. Bake until the cakes are golden and a toothpick inserted in the center comes out clean, 32 to 35 minutes for the 8-inch pans and 40 to 50 minutes for the bowl cake. Transfer the cakes to a wire rack and cool in the pans for 20 minutes. Invert, remove the pans, and cool completely.

3 Trim the top of each cake level. Crumble the trimmings into small pieces and spread them on a cookie sheet. Bake the crumbs until golden and crisp, stirring halfway through, about 10 to 12 minutes. Set aside and cool completely.

4 For the lettuce leaves, sprinkle a work surface with some of the sugar. Roll out the spearmint leaves to a scant ¼-inch thickness, adding more sugar on top to prevent sticking. Cut 2 of the flattened leaves into very small pieces for the pickles in the tartar sauce. Pinch one side of the remaining flattened leaves to give them a lettuce-leaf shape.

5 For the cheese slice, microwave 4 circus peanuts for no more than 3 seconds to soften. Press them together and roll out into a 3-inch square. Trim the edges straight with a sharp knife or scissors. Repeat with the remaining circus peanuts to make 4 squares.

6 Tint 1 can plus ½ cup of the vanilla frosting light brown with the yellow food coloring and cocoa powder. Tint ½ cup of the remaining vanilla frosting pale yellow with the food coloring. For the bottom bun, place the round cake layer on a serving platter and spread some of the light brown frosting on the sides and a thin layer on top and smooth. Arrange 12 of the spearmint leaves, pinched end in, around the top edge for the lettuce.

7 For the fish cake, place the toasted cake crumbs on a plate. Spread the remaining vanilla frosting on the sides of the square cake and a thin layer on top. Press the cake crumbs into the frosting to completely cover. Place the square cake on top of the round cake with the spearmint leaves. Place the circus-peanut cheese on the square cake, allowing a corner of one square of cheese to hang over each side of the cake. For the tartar sauce, spoon some of the pale yellow frosting on top of each cheese slice and sprinkle with some of the chopped spearmint leaves.

8 For the top bun, spread the remaining light brown frosting on the rounded side of the bowl cake and smooth. Place the bowl cake on top of the fish cake layer. Sprinkle the top with the yellow candy-coated sunflower seeds.

9 For the olive, cut a thin slice from the flat end of each green spice drop. Press the flat cut ends together. Remove a ¼-inch square from one rounded end. Cut a ¼-inch rectangle from the red spice drop and insert it into the square opening on the green spice drop as the pimiento. For the toothpick, cut a 1-inch piece from the wheat stick and press it between the two spice drops of the olive. Press the other longer piece of the wheat stick into the opposite side.

10 For more tartar sauce, spoon the remaining pale yellow frosting into the small plastic cups and sprinkle with the remaining chopped spearmint leaves. Just before serving, insert the olive and wheat stick into the top of the cake and place the remaining whole spearmint leaf with the 2 yellow candy fruit slices at the side of the cake.

CHICKEN POT PIE

NO-BAKE • MAKES 5 SMALL CHICKEN PIES

Bite into succulent chunks of chicken slathered in cream sauce with peas, corn, and carrots under a golden crust and . . . April Fool's! It's a trifle made from pound cake with vanilla pudding and bits of candy, topped with a butterscotch candy lattice.

- 1 **recipe Candy Clay (page 230), made with butterscotch chips**
- 1 **bag (6.5 ounces) orange circus peanuts**
- 1 **cup candy corn**
- ¼ **cup small light green jelly beans (Jelly Belly)**
- 2 **tablespoons sweetened flaked coconut, finely chopped**
  Green and yellow food coloring
- 1 **frozen pound cake (16 ounces; Sara Lee Family Size), thawed**
- 2 **cups store-bought vanilla pudding, prepared according to package directions**
- 1 **tablespoon unsweetened cocoa powder**
- 2 **tablespoons warm water**

1 For the lattice, divide the candy clay in half. Roll out half of the clay between two sheets of waxed paper into a 6-inch-long rectangle about ⅛ inch thick. Using a fluted pastry wheel or a paring knife, cut the candy clay lengthwise into ½-inch-wide strips. Repeat with the scraps and the other half of the clay (you will need 40 strips). Cover with plastic wrap to prevent drying.

2 Arrange 4 strips of the candy clay parallel and about 1 inch apart on a sheet of waxed paper. Fold back every other strip halfway. Place a center strip crosswise over the unfolded strips, then replace the folded-back strips. Fold back alternate strips on one side and set the second crosswise strip in place. Repeat on the opposite side to weave a total of 4 crosswise strips into the lattice. At the cross sections, moisten the area under the candy clay with water to secure the lattice. Repeat to make 5 lattice crusts. Keep the lattice covered with plastic wrap to prevent drying.

3 For the carrot slices, cut the circus peanuts in half lengthwise. Flatten each half with a rolling pin and cut out ¾-inch round circles using a cookie cutter or the back of a pastry tip (alternatively, cut the whole circus peanuts into small cubes). For the corn, use a small knife to remove the orange and white parts of the candy corn, keeping the yellow bottom portions. For the peas, cut the jelly beans in half crosswise. For the parsley, place the coconut in a ziplock bag with 3 drops of green and 1 drop of yellow food coloring. Seal the bag and shake vigorously until the coconut is tinted green.

4 For the chicken, cut the pound cake into irregular 1½-inch pieces. Lightly toss the cake with the pudding. Spoon the mixture into five 5-inch pie pans or small, shallow bowls. Sprinkle the candy vegetables on top of the cake-pudding mixture, tucking them into the pudding. Make sure to arrange the jelly beans cut side down. Sprinkle lightly with the coconut parsley.

5 Use a large spatula to transfer the lattice top to each pie. Gently press the candy clay to form it to the cake and pudding filling. Press at the rim to secure, then trim the excess with a paring knife.

6 Dissolve the cocoa powder in the 2 tablespoons warm water. Dip the tip of a firm pastry brush or new toothbrush into the cocoa mixture, hold it over the pies, and run a fork, finger, or chopstick over the bristles to lightly spritz the pies, dipping again when necessary, to make a pattern resembling browned spots on a piecrust. Serve.

april fool's!

COMPOST PIE-L

MAKES 1 COMPOST CAKE; 12 SERVINGS

Going green just got tastier! Our compost pile is a marshmallow and chocolate chip–filled semifreddo topped with chocolate cookie crumbs inside a honey wheat–pretzel fence. Piles of dirt, kitchen scraps, grass, and wood shavings are ready for composting.

COMPOST PILE
Nonstick cooking spray
About 50 honey wheat pretzel sticks (Snyder's)
1¼ **cups graham cracker crumbs**
3 **tablespoons sugar**
5 **tablespoons butter, melted**
2 **cups semisweet chocolate chips (Nestlé, Ghirardelli)**
8 **creme-filled chocolate sandwich cookies (Oreos)**
1 **can (14 ounces) sweetened condensed milk**
1 **container (12 ounces) frozen whipped topping (Cool Whip), thawed**
1 **cup mini marshmallows**
3 **yellow licorice laces (see Sources)**
1 **chocolate graham cracker**
1 **tube (4.25 ounces) yellow decorating icing (Cake Mate)**

1 Preheat the oven to 350°F. Line the bottom of an 8-inch round springform pan with foil. Spray the sides of the pan with nonstick cooking spray.

2 For the fence, using a serrated knife, trim about ¾ inch from one end of each pretzel stick; the sticks should be irregular lengths. Combine the graham cracker crumbs, sugar, and melted butter in a medium bowl. Stir until well blended. Press the crumb mixture into the bottom of the pan. Arrange the pretzel sticks, trimmed end down, along the outer edge of the pan, pressing them into the crumb mixture. Bake until fragrant and golden, about 7 minutes. Transfer to a wire rack, adjust any fallen pretzel sticks, and cool completely.

3 For the compost, microwave 1 cup of the chocolate chips in a large bowl, stirring every 10 seconds, until melted and smooth, about 1 minute. Let cool for about 5 minutes.

4 Cut the cookies into quarters; set aside. Add the condensed milk to the cooled chocolate, stirring until well blended. Fold one third of the whipped topping into the chocolate mixture until well blended. Fold in half of the remaining whipped topping. Add the remaining whipped topping, remaining 1 cup chocolate chips, the mini marshmallows, and the cut-up cookies and fold until evenly distributed. Spoon the mixture into the cooled crust in the pan. Cover the top of the pan with plastic wrap and freeze until set, at least 4 hours or overnight.

5 For the sign, cut one of the licorice laces into a 5-inch length. Cut the chocolate graham cracker in half lengthwise with a serrated knife. Squeeze 1 dot of yellow icing near each end on the back side of one of the graham cracker pieces. Press the ends of the licorice lace into the icing to secure. Turn the graham cracker over. Write the word "compost" on top with the yellow icing.

6 Remove the dessert from the freezer. Carefully run a thin knife around the outside of the pretzel sticks to loosen. Remove the pan and transfer the dessert to a serving platter. Wrap the remaining 2 yellow licorice laces around the dessert and tie in the front. Hang the sign on the side of the dessert. Sprinkle the top of the dessert with some of the dirt and the worms (see opposite page).

7 Serve with the additional compost items in small dishes on the side.

additional compost items

12 **creme-filled chocolate sandwich cookies (Oreos)**
2 **pink fruit chews (Jolly Rancher, Laffy Taffy)**
½ **cup sweetened flaked coconut**
   Green and yellow food coloring
1 **cup cornflakes**
½ **cup canned vanilla frosting**
1 **each red, green, yellow, and orange candy fruit slices**
6 **thin honey wheat sticks (Pringles)**
¼ **cup toffee chips (Heath Toffee Bits)**
½ **cup white chocolate chips (Nestlé, Ghirardelli)**
12 **plastic spoons**
8 **soft caramels (Kraft)**

Dirt: Place the cookies in a food processor and process until finely ground.

Worms: Microwave the fruit chews for no more than 3 seconds to soften. Press the fruit chews together and roll into a 5-inch-long rope. Cut the rope in half and taper each end. Run the back of a paring knife along the rope to make ridges for each worm.

Grass: Place the coconut in a ziplock bag. Add a few drops of the green food coloring. Seal the bag and shake vigorously until the coconut is tinted grass green.

Kitchen scraps: Line a cookie sheet with waxed paper. Place ¾ cup of the cornflakes in a large bowl. Tint the vanilla frosting light green with the green and yellow food coloring. Heat the frosting in the microwave, stirring every 5 seconds, until it has the texture of lightly whipped cream, about 15 seconds. Pour the frosting over the cereal and toss to coat well. Spread the coated cereal on the cookie sheet in an even layer and refrigerate until set, about 20 minutes. Remove a ¼-inch strip from the outer edge of each fruit slice. Cut the strips into ¾-inch pieces. Toss with the coated cereal.

Wood shavings: Break the thin wheat sticks into 1-inch pieces. Combine with the remaining ¼ cup cornflakes and the toffee chips.

Eggshells: Microwave the white chocolate chips in a small bowl, stirring every 10 seconds, until melted and smooth, about 30 seconds. Spread a small amount of the white chocolate on the inside of 12 plastic spoons and place them on a cookie sheet. Refrigerate until set, about 5 minutes. Once they are set, remove the chocolate shells from the spoons and break into large pieces.

Brown paper bags: Unwrap the caramels. Microwave for no more than 3 seconds to soften. Press them together and roll out to a $\frac{1}{16}$-inch thickness on a sheet of waxed paper. Using a fluted pastry wheel or pinking shears, cut the caramel sheet into 1- to 2-inch strips. Fold the caramel pieces to look like paper bags.

Optional: Test your guests by making noncompostable ingredients like steak (pink and white fruit chews), bones (white chocolate), or tires (mini chocolate doughnuts).

SOURPUSSES

MAKES 12 SOURPUSSES

Pucker up and give the Lemon Head Gang a kiss. That's right, Lemon and Lime have a Hershey's Mini Kiss hidden under their rind. Sour Orange has no kiss, but he does have tang. Now that's citrus with appeal.

1 can (16 ounces) plus 1 cup vanilla frosting
8 vanilla cupcakes baked in orange paper liners (see Sources)
8 vanilla cupcakes baked in yellow paper liners (see Sources)
8 vanilla cupcakes baked in green paper liners (see Sources)

RINDS
8 large chocolate chips (Hershey's Mini Kisses)
Red, yellow, and green food coloring
1 cup each orange and yellow decorating sugars (Cake Mate)
1 cup dark green decorating sugar (see Sources)
2 tablespoons light green decorating sugar (see Sources)

FACES
Chocolate chews (Tootsie Rolls)
Yellow, pink, and green fruit chews (Jolly Rancher, Laffy Taffy)
Granulated sugar
Orange, white, and green spice drops
Red, green, and blue licorice laces (see Sources)
Pastel and white flat candies (Smarties)
Flat candy wafers (Necco)
Brown and yellow mini candy-coated chocolates (M&M's Minis)
Fruit cereal O's (Froot Loops)
Orange, yellow, green, and red hard candies (Runts)
Orange and green jelly beans
Thin pretzel sticks (Bachman)
Lemon drops (Brach's)

1 Spoon ¼ cup of the vanilla frosting into a ziplock bag. Press out the excess air and seal the bag.

2 Trim the tops of the cupcakes level with a serrated knife. Remove the liners from four of each color liner (keeping the best-looking of each color intact). Spread some of the remaining vanilla frosting on top of the cupcakes with liners and place an unwrapped cupcake, trimmed side down, on top of each frosted cupcake, pressing down to secure. Round off the joined

edges of the cupcakes with a serrated knife. For the lemons and limes, use a dot of frosting to attach a large chocolate chip to the top of each cupcake with a yellow or green liner. Freeze the cupcakes until firm, about 15 minutes.

3 Divide the remaining vanilla frosting among three bowls. Tint the frostings yellow, green, and orange (use red and yellow together) with the food coloring. Cover the frostings with plastic wrap. Spoon the colored sugars into separate shallow bowls.

4 Working on one frozen cupcake at a time and using the color that matches the liner, spread some of the frosting over the cupcake and smooth. Roll the cupcake in the same color sugar to cover completely. For the green cupcakes, sprinkle the cupcake in a few spots with the light green sugar before rolling in the dark green sugar.

5 For the faces: Microwave several of the chocolate and colored fruit chews at a time for no more than 3 seconds to soften. Roll out the chews to a ⅛-inch thickness. Make beards, mustaches, eyebrows, and tongues by cutting into the desired shapes with scissors or a small knife. For mouths, ears, hat brims, and leaves, sprinkle the work surface with the granulated sugar and roll out some of the spice drops (leave several whole for the tops of the hats), adding sugar as necessary to prevent sticking. Cut into desired shapes (pinch together one end of each leaf). Snip a small (⅛-inch) corner from the bag of vanilla frosting. For eyeglasses and monocles, make a loop in the licorice lace and secure with a dot of frosting. Pipe small dots of vanilla frosting on the cupcakes and attach the candy and cereal face parts, using the photo as a guide.

6 Press the spice drop leaves onto the pretzel sticks. Arrange the sticks and leaves and some lemon drops on the serving platter with the cupcakes.

citrus with appeal

SHRIMP COCKTAIL ON ICE

NO-BAKE • MAKES 8 SHRIMP ON ICE

Instead of starting a dinner party with a shrimp ring from the grocery store, why not end it with pound cake shrimp on gelatin ice? Serve with whipped topping rémoulade sauce. Fancy!

- 4 cups white cranberry juice (Ocean Spray) or white grape juice
- 3 envelopes (0.25 ounce each) unflavored gelatin (Knox)
- ½ cup sugar
- Neon blue, neon pink, yellow, and green food coloring (McCormick)
- 8 pink marshmallows (Kraft Jet-Puffed Strawberry Mallows)
- ¼ cup white chocolate chips (Nestlé, Ghirardelli)
- 16 thin pretzel sticks (Bachman)
- 1 frozen pound cake (16 ounces; Sara Lee Family Size), thawed
- 1 can (16 ounces) vanilla frosting
- 1 cup frozen whipped topping (Cool Whip), thawed
- 1 tablespoon sweetened flaked coconut

OPTIONAL GARNISH
Candy lemon slices
Candy spearmint leaves (Farley's), flattened

1 Have ready two 8-inch square pans. For the ice, place 1 cup of the fruit juice in a medium bowl. Sprinkle the gelatin over the juice and let stand until softened, about 5 minutes.

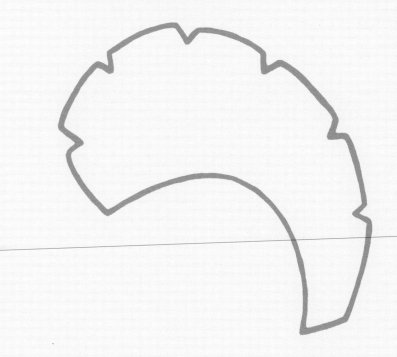

2 Bring the remaining 3 cups juice and the sugar to a simmer in a medium saucepan over medium heat, stirring until the sugar is dissolved. Pour the hot liquid over the gelatin and stir until dissolved. Pour half of the mixture into one of the pans. Tint the remaining mixture with 1 drop of neon blue food coloring. Pour the tinted mixture into the remaining pan. Refrigerate until firm, about 3 hours.

3 Line a cookie sheet with waxed paper. Cut the marshmallows crosswise into thirds with clean scissors. To make the tail shape, press 3 ends together like a fan (see photo). Place the white chocolate chips in a ziplock bag; do not seal the bag. Microwave for 10 seconds to soften. Massage the chips in the bag, return to the microwave, and repeat until the chips are smooth, about 30 seconds. Press out the excess air and seal the bag. Snip a small (⅛-inch) corner from the bag. Pipe some of the white chocolate on the underside of one of the marshmallow tails. Place a pretzel stick in the melted chocolate, allowing it to overhang the bottom of the tail by about 1½ inches. Use another pretzel stick to support the overhanging pretzel while it hardens. Repeat with the remaining pretzels and marshmallow tails. Refrigerate until set, about 5 minutes.

4 Line a cookie sheet with waxed paper and place a wire rack on top. For the shrimp bodies, trim the ends of the pound cake even. Cut the cake crosswise into 8 slices about 1¼ inches thick. Use the template on page 47 and a small knife to cut the shrimp shapes (reserve the scraps for another use). Following the template, cut small notches on the sides of each body, about 1 inch apart, with a small knife to create the shell-segment shapes. Arrange the cake pieces on the rack.

5 Tint ¼ cup of the vanilla frosting dark pink with the neon pink food coloring. Spoon the frosting into a ziplock bag, press out the excess air, and seal the bag. Tint the remaining vanilla frosting light pink. Microwave the light pink frosting, stopping to stir frequently, until it has the texture of lightly whipped cream, 20 to 30 seconds. Microwave the bag with the dark pink frosting, massaging the bag frequently, until it has the texture of lightly whipped cream, 5 to 10 seconds. Spoon some of the light pink frosting over each piece of cake to cover. Gather

the excess frosting up from the waxed paper, reheat, and spoon over the cake, if necessary. Snip a very small (1⁄16-inch) corner from the bag with the dark pink frosting. Drizzle thin lines crosswise over the tops and sides of the cakes (see photo).

6 Squeeze some of the pink food coloring into a small bowl. Dip the bristles of a firm pastry brush or new toothbrush into the color. Spray spots of color onto the cakes and marshmallow tails by running a fork, finger, or chopstick over the bristles. Refrigerate on the wire rack until the frosting is set, about 30 minutes.

7 For the rémoulade sauce, tint the whipped topping with the yellow food coloring. Spoon into little bowls. For the parsley, place the coconut in a ziplock bag with 3 drops green and 1 drop yellow food coloring. Seal the bag and shake vigorously until the coconut is tinted green. Sprinkle the rémoulade with the green coconut.

8 For the ice cubes, dip the bottom of one pan of gelatin into warm water to loosen. Invert the gelatin onto a cutting board. Cut the gelatin into 3⁄4-inch strips and cut the strips crosswise into 3⁄4-inch cubes. Repeat with the other pan of gelatin. Divide some of the cubes among 8 stemmed glasses, adding a few of each color (place any extra cubes in a serving bowl).

9 Loosen the shrimp from the cooling rack with a small spatula. Press the pretzel end of a marshmallow tail into the tapered end of a shrimp. Repeat with the remaining tails and shrimp. Transfer each shrimp to a glass with gelatin cubes. Serve with the rémoulade sauce, garnished with the lemon slices and spearmint leaves, if using.

crafting with chocolate

It's easy to work with chocolate melting wafers and morsels. (Follow the individual recipes for precise melting instructions.)

• **Use melted chocolate as glue to attach treats and add candy details.**

• **Create unique shapes, such as petals, by dipping the back of a plastic spoon into melted white chocolate.**

• **Make chocolate drawings by placing waxed paper over a template and piping along the outlines.**

• **Craft colorful rounded shapes, such as ladybug shells, by placing mini morsels in a plastic spoon and covering them with melted red candy wafers.**

animal planet

Putting the candy before the critter is a bit like the tail wagging the dog. But using marshmallows for fleece, spice drops for feathers, and M&M's for scales makes these animals so easy you'll be done in two shakes of a lamb's tail.

BIG MOUTH FROGS

MAKES 12 CROAKER CUPCAKES

The frogs in this chorus sport mouths as wide as cupcakes. Each is double-sized, with a large slice removed to create the loudest ribbit ever.

- 24   **vanilla cupcakes baked in green paper liners (Reynolds)**
- 2   **cans (16 ounces each) vanilla frosting**
- 24   **pink fruit chews (Jolly Rancher, Laffy Taffy)**
- 2   **rolls (0.75 ounce each) strawberry fruit leather (Fruit by the Foot)**
-   **Green and yellow food coloring**
- ½   **cup green and brown mini candy-coated chocolates (M&M's Minis)**
- 24   **white Jordan almonds**
- 24   **brown candy-coated chocolates (M&M's)**
- 1   **tube (4.25 ounces) chocolate decorating icing (Cake Mate)**
- 1   **tablespoon chocolate sprinkles (optional)**

1 Trim the tops of the cupcakes level with a serrated knife. Remove the liners from 12 of the cupcakes (keep the best-looking ones intact). Spread some of the vanilla frosting on top of each cupcake that has a paper liner. Place an unwrapped cupcake, trimmed side down, on top of the frosting, pressing down to secure. Using a serrated knife, remove a ¾-inch corner from either side of the top cupcakes (see photo). Freeze until firm, about 20 minutes.

2 Spread a thin layer of vanilla frosting over the frozen cupcakes and smooth. Freeze until ready to dip in the frosting.

Trim   Coat   Dip   Cut

3 For the mouths, microwave the pink fruit chews for no more than 3 seconds to soften. Press 2 fruit chews together and roll out into a 3-inch circle. Repeat with the remaining fruit chews. Stack the flattened fruit chews between sheets of waxed paper. For the tongues, unwrap the fruit leather, unroll, and press the 2 strips together, shiny side in, to make a double thickness. Cut the fruit leather into a variety of lengths from 2 to 3 inches (you'll need 12 pieces). Cut a small notch from one short end of each piece.

4 Tint ½ cup of the vanilla frosting dark green with the food coloring and spoon it into a ziplock bag. Spoon ¼ cup of the remaining vanilla frosting into a ziplock bag. Press out the excess air and seal the bags. Tint the remaining vanilla frosting bright green with the green and yellow food coloring. Spoon the bright green frosting into a 2-cup glass measuring cup.

5 Microwave the bright green frosting, stopping to stir frequently, until it has the texture of lightly whipped cream, 25 to 35 seconds. Holding a chilled cupcake by the liner, dip it into the melted frosting up to the liner (see photo). Allow the excess frosting to drip back into the cup. Turn right side up, tap the bottom of the cupcake lightly to flatten the frosting, and let stand. Repeat with the remaining cupcakes. If the frosting begins to thicken while you are dipping, reheat it in the microwave for several seconds, stirring well.

6 Place a cupcake with an untrimmed side facing you (see photo). For the mouth, use a small knife to make a side-to-side cut, close to the top, and remove a wedge 1 to 2 inches deep and ½ to ¾ inch thick straight down into the cupcake. Use a dot of bright green frosting to attach some of the green and brown mini candy-coated chocolates to the cupcakes as warts. Repeat with the remaining cupcakes.

7 Snip a small (⅛-inch) corner from the bags with the dark green and vanilla frosting.

8 For the eyes, insert 2 of the Jordan almonds, narrow end down, into the top of each cupcake. For the mouths, cut the flattened pink fruit chews into semicircles that will fit inside the cut areas on the cupcakes. Secure the pieces with some of the vanilla frosting.

9 Pipe a line of dark green frosting around the almond eyes and the mouth. For the pupils, pipe a dot of vanilla frosting on the almonds and add the brown candy-coated chocolates. Pipe the nostrils with the chocolate decorating icing. Secure the tongue in the mouth opening with a dot of vanilla frosting. Arrange 3 chocolate sprinkles as the eyelashes on either side of the eyes, if desired.

melted frosting

Canned frosting is easy to melt and dries to a smooth, silky coating.

• For dipping, place the frosting in a microwavable measuring cup or a bowl wide and deep enough to hold your treats. For pouring, the depth is not important, but a pouring spout on the lip is helpful.

• Microwave the frosting, stopping every 10 seconds to stir, until it has the texture of lightly whipped cream (15 to 45 seconds total, depending on the volume of frosting; follow the timing in the recipe). When you stir, be sure to incorporate the frosting from the bottom and sides of the cup so it all gets evenly melted.

• The frosting is ready to be used when it can be drizzled from a spoon and incorporates immediately back into the frosting in the cup without piling up.

• Frosting can be tinted. Add food coloring before melting.

pyrex®

1 CUP ◄ 8 oz ► 1 CUP
3/4 ◄ 6 oz ► 2/3
1/2 ◄ 4 oz ► 1/2
1/4 ◄ 2 oz ► 1/3

dipping, pouring, and drizzling

Cookies, cupcakes with liners, and fork bites are good candidates for dipping. Bigger treats and irregular shapes are best coated by pouring the frosting over them.

- Place the treats on waxed paper or a wire rack with waxed paper underneath to catch drips.

- Hold the treat by the liner or one end and dip it into the melted frosting to the desired depth.

- Use a spoon to assist in coating any hard-to-reach areas.

- Lift the treat out and allow the excess frosting to drip off before inverting. Set aside to firm.

- For larger treats, pour or spoon the melted frosting over the treat to cover.

- Create marbleized and spotted patterns by drizzling a second color of frosting on top of the first color while it is still wet.

BAA BAA BLACK SHEEP

NO-BAKE • MAKES 7 SHEEP

Have you any wool? No sir, no sir, just pound cake with mini marshmallows and a Milano cookie head. The black sheep's color comes from a dusting of cocoa powder.

- 1 **frozen pound cake (16 ounces; Sara Lee Family Size), thawed**
- 7 **chocolate-filled butter sandwich cookies (Milano)**
- 1 **can (16 ounces) plus 1 cup vanilla frosting**
- 1 **can (16 ounces) dark chocolate frosting**
- **Black, green, and yellow food coloring (McCormick)**
- ½ **cup sweetened flaked coconut**
- 1 **teaspoon unsweetened cocoa powder**
- 1 **bag (10.5 ounces) mini marshmallows**
- 24 **thin pretzel sticks (Bachman)**
- 1 **tablespoon flower decors (Cake Mate)**
- 14 **mini chocolate chips (Nestlé)**
- 14 **small black jelly beans (Jelly Belly)**
- 7 **pink round decors (Cake Mate)**

1 Trim the ends of the pound cake even. Cut crosswise into 7 pieces, each about 1⅓ inches thick.

2 For the legs and grass, using a small knife, remove a rectangular section of cake 2 inches long by ½ inch deep from the center of the bottom edge of each slice (see photo). Reserve the 7 pieces for the patches of grass.

3 For the heads, use a serrated knife to trim ¼ inch on the diagonal from either side of one short end of each cookie (see photo).

discard

body

head

patch of grass

4 Tint 1 tablespoon of the vanilla frosting with 1 teaspoon of the dark chocolate frosting. Spoon into a ziplock bag. Tint the remaining dark chocolate frosting black with the food coloring. Spoon ¾ cup of the black frosting and ¼ cup of the vanilla frosting into separate ziplock bags, press out the excess air, and seal the bags. Tint ½ cup of the remaining vanilla frosting grass green with the green and yellow food coloring.

5 Place the coconut in a ziplock bag with 3 drops green and 1 drop yellow food coloring. Seal the bag and shake vigorously until the coconut is tinted green. Place the coconut in a shallow bowl.

6 Place the cocoa powder in a ziplock bag with 1 cup of the mini marshmallows. Seal the bag and shake vigorously until the marshmallows are completely covered. For the tails, cut 3 white marshmallows and 1 cocoa-coated marshmallow in half on the diagonal. For the wool on the head, cut 18 white and 3 cocoa-coated marshmallows in half crosswise. Dip the cut sides of the heads and tails in the cocoa powder. Cover the marshmallows with plastic wrap to prevent drying.

7 Line two cookie sheets with waxed paper. Place the remaining black frosting in a shallow bowl and heat in the microwave, stopping to stir frequently, until it has the texture of lightly whipped cream, 15 to 20 seconds. Holding a trimmed cookie at the narrow end, dip it into the melted frosting to cover completely, allowing the excess frosting to drip back into the bowl. Transfer the cookie to a cookie sheet. Repeat with the remaining cookies. If the frosting becomes too thick, microwave for several seconds and stir.

8 Hold a cake slice, trimmed side down, and dip it into the melted frosting to ½ inch above the cut-out area, allowing the excess frosting to drip back into the bowl. Transfer the cake to the cookie sheet with the cookies, standing the pieces up on their legs. Repeat with the remaining cake slices. Refrigerate the cookies and cake pieces until set, about 30 minutes.

9 For the fence, snip a small (⅛-inch) corner from the bags with the frostings. Place 2 pretzel sticks parallel on the remaining prepared cookie sheet about 2 inches apart. Pipe a dot of the black frosting ¾ inch from one end of each pretzel stick and another dot ¾ inch from the first dot. Place 2 pretzel sticks crosswise, attaching with the dots of frosting (see photo, page 60). Repeat with the remaining pretzel sticks. Set aside until firm, about 20 minutes.

10 For the grass patches, spread some of the green frosting over the reserved cake pieces to cover. Sprinkle the tops of the pieces with the green coconut and the flower decors. Carefully insert a pretzel fence upright into all but one piece, adding more black frosting to the pretzels to secure, if necessary.

11 To assemble the sheep, carefully remove the cookies and cake from the waxed paper, trimming off any excess frosting. For the wool, spread some of the remaining vanilla frosting over the sides and top of a cake slice. Press whole white marshmallows all over the sides and top of the cake, leaving an opening at one end uncovered for the head. Arrange a dipped cookie in the opening as the head, narrow end up, allowing one third of the cookie to hang over the side and pressing it into the frosting to secure. Pipe some vanilla frosting at the top of the cookie head and attach 6 white marshmallow halves. Pipe a dot of frosting at the backside and attach the marshmallow tail. For the eyes, pipe 2 dots of vanilla frosting onto the cookie. For the pupils, attach 1 mini chocolate chip, flat side out, to each dot of frosting. For the ears, pipe a dot of the black frosting on either side of the cookie and attach a jelly bean. For the tongue, press a pink decor into the frosting at the bottom edge of the cookie. Pipe the nostrils with the chocolate-tinted vanilla frosting. Repeat with the remaining cake slices and cookies to make 6 white sheep. For the black sheep, frost the remaining cake piece with the black frosting, then follow the instructions, but using the cocoa-coated marshmallows. Lightly tap the coated marshmallows to remove excess cocoa before attaching.

12 Using a spatula, transfer the sheep and grass patches to a serving platter.

have you any wool?

POLLY WANT A CUPCAKE

MAKES 2 PARROTS; 11 CUPCAKES

Talking to your cupcakes could make you go crackers. But Polly looks so real it's hard to resist. The plumage is made from rolled spice drops, but it's the cashews used for the beaks and claws that lend this bird a super-realistic look. "Say pretty bird, pretty bird."

½ cup light green decorating sugar (see Sources)

14 green, 8 white, and 4 red spice drops

3 tablespoons red decorating sugar (Cake Mate)

1 can (16 ounces) vanilla frosting

Yellow and green food coloring

11 vanilla cupcakes baked in foil liners (Reynolds)

8 whole cashews

2 brown mini candy-coated chocolates (M&M's Minis)

1 tablespoon yellow sprinkles

1 plain bread stick (9½ inches long)

1 For the feathers, sprinkle a work surface with some of the light green sugar. Place a green spice drop on the surface, sprinkle with additional sugar, and roll out the candy to a rough oval about 2 inches long and ⅛ inch thick, sprinkling with more sugar if necessary to prevent sticking. Repeat with the remaining green and white spice drops. Repeat the process with the red sugar and red spice drops.

2 Line a cookie sheet with waxed paper. Cut the rolled-out green and white spice drops into 1-by-2¼-inch pieces, tapered at each end, to make 22 green feathers. Cut the red spice drops into 1-by-2¼-inch teardrop shapes to make 4 feathers. Transfer the feathers to the cookie sheet.

3 Spoon 2 tablespoons of the vanilla frosting into a ziplock bag. Tint ½ cup of the remaining vanilla frosting yellow with the food coloring and spoon into a ziplock bag. Press out the excess air and seal the bags. Tint the remaining vanilla frosting dark green with the food coloring.

4 Arrange the cupcakes on a large wire rack over a serving platter (see photo): 1 cupcake (as the head), 2 cupcakes (as the wings), 1 cupcake as the body, and 1 cupcake (as the tail), to make one parrot. Repeat to make the other parrot.

5 Working on one parrot at a time, spread the tops of 5 cupcakes with the dark green frosting and smooth. For the head, snip a small (⅛-inch) corner from the bags with the white and yellow frostings. For the beak, pipe a 1-inch dot of vanilla frosting on one side of the head cupcake. Attach 2 whole cashews, the top one curving down and the bottom one curving up, with the larger end pressing into the vanilla frosting. Pipe yellow frosting feathers, starting at the top edge of the head cupcake and, working inward, using the squeeze-release-pull technique (see page 75), cover the top two thirds of the cupcake. Pipe a dot of vanilla frosting and attach a brown candy for the eye. Arrange the spice-drop feathers (see photo, page 63), 3 green for each wing, 5 green for the tail feathers, and 1 red feather for each wing. Repeat for the other parrot, placing the cashew beak on the opposite side of the head so the parrots face each other.

6 Trim ½ inch from one side of the remaining cupcake. Pipe some of the remaining yellow frosting on top and smooth. Top with the yellow sprinkles. Place the yellow frosted cupcake between the parrots, cut side down, as the seed bowl. For the perch, arrange the bread stick across the top of the tail cupcakes. For the feet, press the remaining whole cashews into the body cupcakes, curving over the bread stick.

pretty bird, pretty bird

DOG POUND CAKE

NO-BAKE • MAKES 1 LOVABLE PUP; 10 SERVINGS

When we say "pound," we mean cake, of course. Fido's head, body, and tail are carved from a single store-bought loaf. And his markings, made by flooding the pound cake with vanilla frosting, then spooning over chocolate frosting, hit the spot. This dessert is no-bark and no-bake.

1 **can (16 ounces) plus 1 cup vanilla frosting**
1 **can (16 ounces) milk chocolate frosting**
  Red and blue food coloring
1 **frozen pound cake (16 ounces; Sara Lee Family Size), thawed**
8 **small round brownies (Entenmann's Little Bites)**
1 **tablespoon light pink decorating sugar (see Sources)**
1 **marshmallow**
1 **each large black, red, and yellow spice drops**
1 **roll (0.75 ounce) strawberry fruit leather (Fruit by the Foot)**
2 **drinking straws, cut in half**
2 **brown candy-coated chocolates (M&M's)**
2 **dessert shell cakes (3-inch diameter)**
¼ **cup chocolate cereal O's (Chocolate Cheerios)**

1 Spoon 1½ cups of the vanilla frosting into a ziplock bag. Spoon 1 cup of the chocolate frosting into a ziplock bag. Press out the excess air and seal the bags. Tint ⅓ cup of the remaining vanilla frosting red with the food coloring. Tint 2 tablespoons of the remaining vanilla frosting light blue with the food coloring. Cover the tinted frostings with plastic wrap to prevent drying.

2 Place the pound cake, one long side facing you, on a work surface. For the head, cut a 3-inch piece from one short end of the cake. For the tail, cut a 1-inch piece from the opposite short end. Place the head piece on the work surface, short end facing you, and cut a ⅓-inch piece, angled from either side to taper (see photo). Place the tail piece cut side down on the work surface and cut from corner to corner on the diagonal (one piece is extra).

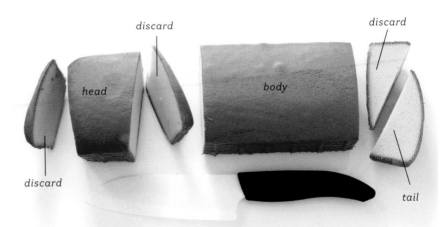

discard

discard

head

body

discard

tail

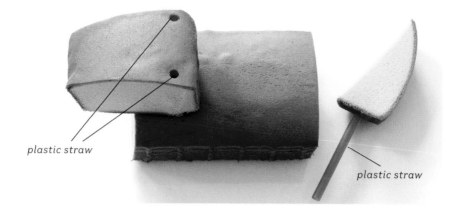

plastic straw

plastic straw

3 Line a cookie sheet with waxed paper and place a wire rack on top. Place the head piece on the body, allowing the tapered end to hang over the edge by 1½ inches. Insert two of the straw pieces straight down into both cakes at the back corners of the head where the ears will be placed (if any straw is exposed, trim it with scissors; see photo). Insert a straw piece into the large end of the tail piece. Place the head and body pieces of cake on the rack. Microwave the remaining vanilla and milk chocolate frostings in separate bowls, stopping to stir frequently, until they have the texture of lightly whipped cream, 20 to 25 seconds. Working with the vanilla frosting, spoon melted frosting over the cake to cover (don't worry too much about the bottom edges; they will be covered with piped frosting later). Spoon some of the chocolate frosting over the cake pieces to make patches. Refrigerate until the frosting is set, about 30 minutes.

4 For the paws, spread some of the remaining chocolate frosting on the large end of 4 of the brownie bites. Sandwich with another brownie bite, large ends together. For the ears, place the pink sugar in a shallow bowl. Cut the marshmallow in half on the diagonal. Press the sticky sides of the marshmallow in the pink sugar to coat. For the nose, place the black spice drop flat side down and trim ¼ inch from one side. Place the spice drop cut side down and remove 1 small semicircle from each side of the rounded end to make the nostrils. For the tongue and tag, cut ¼ inch from the flat end of the red and yellow spice drops. For the collar, unwrap the fruit leather and fold in half, pressing together, to make a double thickness.

5 Snip a medium (¼-inch) corner from the bags with the vanilla and chocolate frostings. Use a large spatula to transfer the cake pieces to a work surface. Pipe some of the chocolate frosting on top of the body piece near one short end. Attach the unfrosted tail at the opposite end of the body.

6 For the collar, wrap the fruit leather around the base of the head, trimming any excess. Pipe a dot of chocolate frosting at the front and attach the yellow spice drop for the tag, cut side in. Attach the marshmallow ears with more chocolate frosting, sugared side out. Arrange the brownie paws on a serving platter, positioned approximately where the 4 corners of the body cake will be. Pipe a dot of chocolate frosting on top of each paw. Using a large spatula, transfer the cake to rest on top of the paws. Adjust the brownies as needed to support the cake.

7 Starting at the base of the body, pipe short vertical lines of the vanilla and chocolate frosting, always pulling down with the frosting, all around the cake. Pipe several rows, overlapping slightly, for the fur. Starting at the tip of the tail, pipe short overlapping lines of vanilla and chocolate frosting, always pulling up. Pipe vertical lines of the frosting to cover the white parts of the marshmallow ears. Pipe several small tufts of frosting in front of the ears. For the muzzle fur, pipe longer vertical lines with the frostings on either side of the front end of the head. Add the red spice drop for the tongue, cut side in, and press on the black spice drop for the nose. Attach the brown candies for the eyes and pipe a few dots of frosting around the eyes for eyelashes.

8 For the dog bowls, line a cookie sheet with waxed paper. Microwave the red frosting in a bowl, stopping to stir frequently, until it has the texture of lightly whipped cream, 5 to 10 seconds. Spoon the red frosting over the cup side of the dessert shells to cover the rim and sides, allowing the excess frosting to drip back into the bowl. Place the coated dessert shells on the cookie sheet. Refrigerate until set, about 30 minutes.

9 Place the chilled dessert shells next to the dog cake. Microwave the light blue frosting in a bowl, stopping to stir frequently, until it has the texture of lightly whipped cream, about 3 seconds. Spoon the blue frosting into one of the dessert shells for the water. For the kibble, add the chocolate cereal to the remaining shell.

RAINBOW TROUT

MAKES 1 SCHOOL OF 12 FISH CUPCAKES

It's the oldest fish tale in the world: orange fish meets green fish, and magic happens. Colorful cupcakes decorated with M&M's and spice drops frolic in gelatin waves made by chilling a layer of blue Jell-O, then topping it with green Jell-O.

BLUE-GREEN WAVES

2 envelopes (0.25 ounce each) unflavored gelatin (Knox)
2 boxes (3 ounces each) blue gelatin dessert (Jell-O)
2 boxes (3 ounces each) green gelatin dessert (Jell-O)

RAINBOW FISH

3 tablespoons blue decorating sugar (Cake Mate)
9 white, 9 orange, 6 yellow, 6 red, and 6 green spice drops
½ cup granulated sugar
1 can (16 ounces) vanilla frosting
Yellow, red, and green food coloring
12 vanilla cupcakes baked in foil liners (Reynolds)
12 thin pretzel sticks (Bachman)
About 60 each red, green, blue, orange, and yellow candy-coated chocolates (M&M's)
24 red and 12 brown mini candy-coated chocolates (M&M's Minis)
1 yellow gummy worm

1 **WAVES:** Place ¼ cup cold water in each of two separate medium bowls. Sprinkle 1 envelope unflavored gelatin over each bowl of water. Let stand for 5 minutes.

2 Pour 2 cups boiling water into each bowl with the unflavored gelatin. Add the 2 boxes of like-colored gelatin to each bowl. Stir until the gelatin is dissolved. Add 1 cup ice to each bowl and stir until dissolved. Set the green gelatin aside (do not refrigerate).

3 Pour the blue gelatin into a 9-by-13-inch baking pan. Refrigerate until just set, about 45 minutes. Gently spoon the still-liquid green gelatin on top of the blue gelatin. Return to the refrigerator until completely set, at least 3 hours.

4 **RAINBOW FISH:** For the fins and tails, sprinkle a work surface with some of the blue sugar. Press 3 of the white spice drops together and sprinkle with additional sugar. Roll out the spice drops to make a 2-inch circle about ⅛ inch thick, sprinkling with more sugar if necessary to prevent sticking. Repeat with the remaining white spice drops and blue sugar. Repeat the process with the orange, yellow, red, and green spice drops, rolling in the granulated sugar.

5 Cut each flattened spice drop disk into one 2-inch and two 1-inch triangles. Cut the long side of the triangles with pinking shears. Pinch the corner of the triangles opposite the pinked edge to shape. Using scissors, give one small triangle a curve at the top for the dorsal fin. Set aside.

6 Spoon 2 tablespoons of the vanilla frosting into a ziplock bag. Press out the excess air and seal the bag. Tint half of the remaining frosting orange with the yellow and red food coloring and the other half green with the green food coloring. Cover the frosting with plastic wrap to prevent drying.

7 Working with 1 color frosting at a time, spread some of the frosting on top of a cupcake and smooth. To support the tail, press a pretzel stick into the cupcake on an angle at one edge, allowing it to hang over the cupcake by ¾ inch. Using coordinating colors of spice drops and M&M's (see photo), insert the pinched end of a large spice-drop tail into the frosting, using the pretzel stick as support. Starting at the tail end, arrange the large candy-coated chocolates as the scales in 4 or 5 rows, overlapping slightly. Press 2 red mini chocolates on the opposite side of the cupcake for the lips. Snip a small (⅛-inch) corner from the bag with the vanilla frosting. Pipe a dot of vanilla frosting for the eye and add a brown mini chocolate as the pupil. Add a small fin of the matching color to the center and a dorsal fin at the top. Repeat with the remaining cupcakes to make 6 orange and 6 green fish.

8 When you are ready to serve, dip the bottom of the pan with the gelatin in warm water to loosen. Invert onto a cutting board. Cut the gelatin lengthwise into ¾-inch-wide strips. Arrange on a platter with the fish cupcakes. Add the gummy worm for bait.

SOCK MONKEY

MAKES 24 CUPCAKES

The tweed knit on this old-fashioned sock toy is made by letting two colors of frosting blend as they are piped in circular swirls. Add a few candies for more fun than a barrel of monkeys.

 1 can (16 ounces) chocolate frosting
 1 can (16 ounces) vanilla frosting
 3 red fruit chews (Jolly Rancher)
 1 piece (2 inches long) red licorice bundle (Twizzlers Pull 'n' Peel)
 1 thin pretzel stick (Bachman)
 6 blue fruit chews (Jolly Rancher)
24 vanilla cupcakes baked in white paper liners
 4 thin chocolate cookies (Famous Chocolate Wafers)
 2 brown mini candy-coated chocolates (M&M's Minis)
 2 chocolate-covered mints (Junior Mints)

1 Spoon ¼ cup of the chocolate frosting into a ziplock bag. Spoon 1¼ cups of the vanilla frosting into a ziplock bag. Spoon half of the remaining vanilla frosting into one side of a ziplock bag and half of the remaining chocolate frosting into the other side (see photo, page 74). Repeat with the remaining vanilla and chocolate frosting to make a second two-color bag. Press out the excess air and seal the bags.

2 Line a cookie sheet with waxed paper. For the lips and tassel, microwave the red fruit chews for no more than 3 seconds to soften. Press together 2 of the fruit chews and roll out on a work surface to make a 3-by-1½-inch oval. Trim the top of the oval slightly to make the lip shape. Use the back of a small knife to make a lengthwise crease. Transfer to the cookie sheet. For the tassel, roll out the remaining red fruit chew to make a 2-by-1-inch rectangle. Wrap the fruit chew around the bottom ½ inch of the licorice bundle, pressing to secure. Peel apart the top part of the licorice strands to loosen. Press the pretzel stick into the fruit chew at the bottom of the tassel (the pretzel will be inserted into the hat cupcake once assembled).

3 For the bow, microwave the blue fruit chews for no more than 3 seconds to soften. Press 3 fruit chews together and roll out to a 4½-by-1¼-inch rectangle. Trim the long sides straight with clean scissors. Cut in half lengthwise into 2 strips. Repeat with the remaining 3 blue fruit chews. Cut a V-shaped notch from the end of 2 strips. Gather the scraps and shape into a small ball. Make a loop with each of the 2 remaining strips and pinch the ends. Press the 2 pinched ends together to make a figure eight and add the 2 strips with the notched ends below as the tails of the bow. Place the fruit chew ball in the center (see photo). Transfer the bow to the cookie sheet with the lips.

4 Arrange the cupcakes on a large serving platter, placing 2 cupcakes side by side for the head with 1 cupcake above for the hat and 1 cupcake below for the mouth, 4 rows of 2 cupcakes side by side for the body, 2 cupcakes on either side of the body for the arms and 1 cupcake for each hand, 2 cupcakes on either side for the legs and feet, and 2 cupcakes for the tail (see photo, page 73).

5 Snip a small (⅛-inch) corner from the bags with the frostings. Pipe some of the chocolate frosting on the cookies and place them, frosting side down, on the tops of the cupcakes, bridging any gaps in the body and head (see photo below).

6 Starting with one of the mixed chocolate and vanilla frosting bags and using a circular motion, pipe horizontal rows of frosting to cover the 8 body cupcakes, the 2 side head cupcakes, the lower third of the hat cupcake, the 4 arm cupcakes, the top third of the hand cupcakes, the 2 leg cupcakes, the top third of the foot cupcakes, and half of the tail cupcake nearest the body (see photo, page 73). Using the same circular motion, pipe the vanilla frosting over the remaining unfrosted cupcakes. Pipe a second row of vanilla frosting on the hat cupcake to look like the brim of the hat.

7 Place the lips and bow fruit chews on top of the cupcakes, using the photo as a guide. Add the mini chocolates for the nostrils and the mints for the eyes. Pipe 4 small dots of chocolate frosting on top of each mint to look like buttonholes. Just before serving, poke a hole in the side of the hat cupcake with a toothpick and insert the pretzel part of the tassel, adding some frosting to secure if necessary.

piping

Perfect piping starts with a freezer-weight ziplock bag (avoid the ones with expandable bottoms; they don't have pointed corners).

- **To pipe peaks, use a squeeze-release-pull technique. Snip a small (⅛-inch) corner from the ziplock bag. Touch the tip of the bag to the surface of the treat and squeeze to anchor the frosting. As you stop squeezing, pull the tip away from the surface. Squeezing less gives you a smaller peak; squeezing more and continuing to squeeze while pulling the tip away makes bigger peaks.**

- **Invert the bag over your hand and press to make a cup inside your fingers. Fill the cup with frosting and then lift the edges of the bag up and around the frosting. Press out the excess air and seal the bag.**

- **To pipe a line, snip a very small (¹⁄₁₆-inch) corner from the ziplock bag. Touch the tip of the bag to the surface of the treat and begin squeezing. Continue to squeeze as you lift the tip away from the surface, creating a line of frosting in the air as it flows from the tip. As you continue squeezing, the line will settle onto the surface. When the line is the right length, drop the tip back down to the surface to anchor it and stop squeezing. You can use this technique to make straight lines like X's, or you can direct the line to make curves.**

- **For marbleized patterns, place two colors of frosting in the ziplock bag, one color on one side of the bottom corner and another color on the other side. Snip a small (⅛-inch) corner from the ziplock bag and pipe. The frosting will come out with a mix of the two colors.**

- **To make a knitted pattern, pipe the frosting in rows of small overlapping loops.**

MOO PIES AND UDDER THINGS

MAKES 12 SANDWICH COOKIES

The bovine spots on these udderly delicious chocolate sandwich cookies with a fluffy filling come from flooding the cookie with vanilla frosting, then adding drips of dark chocolate frosting before the vanilla sets up.

  1 box (18.25 ounces) chocolate cake mix
  1 large egg
  8 tablespoons (1 stick) butter, melted
  6 chocolate chews (Tootsie Rolls)
  3 yellow Swedish fish
  6 orange and 24 brown mini candy-coated chocolates (M&M's Minis)
  1 can (16 ounces) vanilla frosting
    Neon pink and black food coloring (McCormick)
  ¼ cup canned dark chocolate frosting
  6 pink cereal O's (Froot Loops)
 18 pink licorice pastels (Good & Plenty)
 1½ cups marshmallow creme (Marshmallow Fluff)
 12 yellow banana-shaped hard candies (Runts)

1 In a large bowl, mix the cake mix with the egg and melted butter using an electric mixer. Mix until well blended (the dough may be crumbly). Shape the dough into a 6-inch log on a sheet of waxed paper. Cover with the waxed paper and refrigerate until firm, about 1 hour.

2 Preheat the oven to 350°F. Line three cookie sheets with parchment paper. Unwrap the dough and cut into 24 slices, each about ¼ inch thick. Transfer the slices to the cookie sheets about 1 inch apart. Reshape the slices to make them as round as possible. Bake in batches until the cookies are firm to the touch, 10 to 12 minutes. Transfer to a wire rack to cool completely.

3 For the ears, microwave the chocolate chews for no more than 3 seconds to soften. Roll out each chew on a work surface into a 2-inch oval. Cut each oval into 2 teardrop shapes. For the bells, cut the Swedish fish in half crosswise and press an orange mini chocolate on the cut side to secure.

4 Line two cookie sheets with waxed paper and place wire racks on top. Place 12 of the cookies on the wire racks.

5 Spoon 2 tablespoons of the vanilla frosting into a ziplock bag. Tint ½ cup of the remaining vanilla frosting pink with the food coloring. Spoon the pink frosting into a ziplock bag. Tint the dark chocolate frosting black with the food coloring and spoon it into a ziplock bag. Press out the excess air and seal the bags. Spoon the remaining vanilla frosting into a small bowl. Microwave the black frosting in the bag and the vanilla frosting in the bowl, stopping to massage the bag and stir the frosting in the bowl frequently, until it has the texture of lightly whipped cream, about 5 seconds for the bag and 20 seconds for the bowl.

6 Snip a small (⅛-inch) corner from the bag with the black frosting. Working on one cookie at a time, spoon a generous tablespoon of the melted vanilla frosting on top of a cookie on the wire rack, spreading it to the edges in an irregular pattern. Pipe several spots of the black frosting on top of the vanilla frosting. Tap the rack lightly to flatten the frosting. Continue with the remaining 11 cookies. If the frosting becomes too thick to pour, return to the microwave for 5 seconds, stirring well. Refrigerate until set, about 30 minutes.

7 Snip a small (⅛-inch) corner from the bags with the vanilla and pink frostings. For the faces, pipe the pink frosting into a 1½-inch oval on the lower half of 6 of the frosted cookies for the noses. For the nostrils, press 2 brown mini candies, short side down, into the pink frosting at an angle. Add a cereal O as the tongue. For the eyes, pipe 2 dots of the vanilla frosting and add the remaining brown candies, flat side down. For the udders, pipe pink frosting on the lower third of the remaining 6 frosted cookies and add 3 of the pink licorice pastels to each.

8 Just before serving, spread some of the marshmallow creme on the flat side of the remaining 12 cookies. Sandwich the decorated cookies on top. For the horns, press 2 of the banana candies into the marshmallow creme at the top of the head cookies. Insert the chocolate chew ears to the left and right of the horns. Press a Swedish-fish bell into the marshmallow creme on the lower part of each head cookie sandwich. Arrange the head and body cookies on a serving platter.

CHOCOLATE LADYBUGS

MAKES 24 MINI CUPCAKES

Here's to the ladies who lunch: aren't they a treat? To make a spoonful of chocolate ladybug, place mini chocolate chips in a plastic spoon and add melted red candy wafers on top. Pop them out, add a string of pearls, and the ladies are ready for tea.

24 plastic soupspoons
½ cup mini chocolate chips (Nestlé)
1½ cups red candy melting wafers (Wilton)
1 cup sweetened flaked coconut
Green and yellow food coloring
1 cup vanilla frosting
½ cup dark chocolate frosting
2 tablespoons milk chocolate frosting
24 mini vanilla cupcakes baked in white paper liners
24 chocolate-covered mints (Junior Mints)
¼ cup white candy pearls (see Sources)
24 red mini heart-shaped decors (Wilton)
2 tablespoons chocolate sprinkles
24 mini green paper liners (see Sources)

1 Line a cookie sheet with waxed paper. For the ladybug bodies, line up the plastic spoons on the cookie sheet, bowl side up. Arrange 5 to 7 mini chocolate chips, flat side down, inside the bowl of each spoon. Place the red candy melts in a ziplock bag (do not seal the bag). Microwave for 10 seconds to soften. Massage the wafers in the bag, return to the microwave, and repeat the process until the candy is smooth, about 1 minute. Press out the excess air and seal the bag.

2 Snip a small (⅛-inch) corner from the bag and pipe some of the melted candy into the bowl of a spoon to cover the chips (see photo, page 80). Lightly tap the back of the spoon to flatten the candy. Repeat with the remaining spoons and melted candy. Refrigerate the spoons until the candy is firm, about 7 minutes. When the candy is set, carefully bend the bowls of the spoons to release the candy. (The ladybug bodies can be made up to 1 week in advance and kept in an airtight container.)

3 Pulse the coconut in a food processor until finely chopped. Transfer the coconut to a ziplock bag. Add some green and a drop of yellow food coloring. Seal the bag and shake vigorously until the coconut is tinted grass green. Place the coconut in a shallow bowl.

4 Spoon ¼ cup of the vanilla frosting into a ziplock bag. Spoon the dark chocolate and milk chocolate frostings into separate ziplock bags. Press out the excess air and seal the bags. Tint the remaining vanilla frosting green with the green food coloring and a few drops of yellow.

5 Spread the top of a mini cupcake with the green frosting and smooth. Roll the edge of the cupcake in the coconut. Repeat with the remaining cupcakes.

6 Snip a small (⅛-inch) corner from the bags with the vanilla and dark chocolate frostings. Snip a very small (1⁄16-inch) corner from the bag with the milk chocolate frosting. Pipe a dot of dark chocolate frosting on top of a cupcake. Attach a ladybug body, rounded side up, on top, pressing into the frosting to secure. Pipe 3 dark chocolate legs on either side of the candy body. For the head, pipe a dot of vanilla frosting on one end of the candy body and attach a mint. Pipe a thin line of vanilla frosting around the bottom edge of the mint and attach a row of the candy pearls. Repeat with the remaining cupcakes.

7 Pipe a thin line of milk chocolate frosting down the length of the candy body. For the mouth, attach the heart-shaped decor to the mint with some of the milk chocolate frosting. For the eyes, pipe 2 dots of vanilla frosting onto the mint and attach mini chocolate chips, flat side out, to the frosting for the pupils. For the lashes, add 2 chocolate sprinkles on each eye. Repeat with the remaining cupcakes.

8 Cut zigzag edges from the mini green liners to look like grass. Place a finished ladybug cupcake into each green liner.

HEN HOUSE PIES

NO-BAKE • MAKES 12 HEN PIES

Look who laid an egg—in fact, dozens of them! Fluffy birds, made from whipped topping and licorice, sit on feathered nests of no-bake coconut cream pie. Make plenty, because these birds are so tasty they will be flying the coop as soon as they are made.

12 mini graham cracker crusts (Keebler Ready Crust)
½ teaspoon coconut extract
4 cups store-bought vanilla pudding, prepared according to package directions
2 cups sweetened flaked coconut
   Yellow food coloring
1 orange and 1 red licorice twist (Rainbow Twizzlers)
2 containers (8 ounces each) frozen whipped topping (Cool Whip), thawed
24 mini chocolate chips (Nestlé)
½ cup small white jelly beans (Jelly Belly)

1 Place the crusts on a cookie sheet. Stir the coconut extract into the vanilla pudding. Spoon about ½ cup of the pudding into each mini crust. Refrigerate until ready to use.

2 Preheat the oven to 350°F. Place the coconut in a ziplock bag with some yellow food coloring. Seal the bag. Shake the bag vigorously until the coconut is tinted yellow. Spread the tinted coconut on a cookie sheet in an even layer. Toast the coconut, stirring every few minutes, until it is golden, 7 to 10 minutes. Transfer the pan to a wire rack to cool completely.

3 Cut the orange licorice into twelve ¾-inch triangles with scissors. Cut the red licorice crosswise into 36 thin slices with scissors (see photo).

4 For the nests, sprinkle the edges of the mini pies with some of the toasted coconut.

5 For the hens, divide the whipped topping among four ziplock bags. Press out the excess air and seal the bags. Working with 1 bag at a time, keeping the other bags refrigerated, snip a ½-inch corner from the bag. For the body, pipe a large dollop of whipped topping in the center of a pie, allowing the topping to form a peak at one end for the tail, using the squeeze-release-pull technique (see page 75). For the head, pipe a smaller dollop of topping on the

opposite end from the peak. Using the squeeze-release-pull technique, pipe a whipped-topping wing with a peak on either side of the head (see photo).

6 For the beak, press an orange licorice triangle, pointed end out, in the center of the head. Add 2 red licorice slices as the hen's wattle and 1 piece at the top as the comb. Press 2 mini chocolate chips, pointed end in, into the whipped topping for the eyes. Add a few white jelly beans around the rim of the pie for the eggs. Repeat with the remaining pies, whipped topping, and candies.

7 Arrange the pies on a serving platter, adding the remaining toasted coconut hay and jelly-bean eggs.

PROUD AS A PEACOCK

MAKES 1 FANCY BIRD; 20 SERVINGS

You'd spread your feathers, too, if they were as pretty as the ones on this peafowl. The "eyes" in the feathers are made by rolling out a log of purple candy clay and covering it with a layer of turquoise. Slicing the log reveals the beautiful jeweled colors.

- 1 recipe Candy Clay made with white chocolate chips (page 230)
   Green, yellow, neon blue, and neon purple food coloring (see Sources)
- 1 can (16 ounces) plus 1 cup vanilla frosting
- 1 recipe Perfect Cake Mix (page 224), made with yellow cake and baked as one 8-inch round cake and 11 standard cupcakes in green and blue paper liners (Reynolds)
- 1 S-shaped breakfast treat cookie (Stella D'oro)
- 1 brown mini candy-coated chocolate (M&M's Minis)
- 1 yellow banana-shaped hard candy (Runts), halved crosswise
- 3 dark chocolate–coated wheat sticks (Pocky)

1 Tint 1½ tablespoons of the candy clay neon purple with the food coloring. Tint 2½ tablespoons of the clay neon blue with the food coloring. Divide the remaining clay in half. Tint one half of the clay light green with the yellow and green food coloring. Tint the remaining half darker green with the green and yellow food coloring. Knead each color on a clean work surface until smooth and colors are well incorporated. Keep the clay covered with plastic wrap to prevent drying.

2 Shape the purple clay into a ½-inch-diameter rope 5 inches long. Pinch the rope along one side to form a teardrop-shaped log (see photo). Roll the blue clay between 2 sheets of waxed paper into a 2-by-5-inch rectangle. Place the purple rope on top of the blue rectangle, rounded side down, and wrap the blue clay around the log to cover, pinching to seal edges (see photo). Roll the light green clay into a 1¼-inch-diameter log. Cut the log down to 6 inches and reserve the extra light green clay. Pinch log along one side to form a teardrop-shaped log. Roll ½ cup of the darker green clay between 2 sheets of waxed paper to a 5½-by-6-inch rectangle. Place the light green log on top of the dark green rectangle, rounded side down, and cover with the dark green clay, pinching to seal edges (see photo). Roll the reserved light green clay into a 1-inch oval log. Roll the remaining darker green clay into a 1¾-inch oval log. Cover the logs with plastic wrap to prevent drying.

3 Line two cookie sheets with waxed paper. Using a thin sharp knife, cut the purple log into ⅛-inch-thick slices, reshaping as necessary to maintain the teardrop shape. You will need about 22 slices for the eyes of the feathers, plus 3 additional slices you will reserve for the head feathers. Cut the double-green log into ⅛-inch-thick slices, reshaping as necessary to maintain a teardrop shape. You should get about 40 slices. Working with 22 of the green slices, use a small knife or teardrop-shaped cookie cutter close in size to the purple log slices to remove a piece of clay from the center of the light green clay. Replace with a purple slice (see photo). Roll out the remaining double-green slices and the slices with the purple eyes to lengthen and adhere the clays. Trim edge of flattened candy with pinking shears to look like feathers. Transfer feathers to the cookie sheets. You should have 22 feathers with purple centers and 18 double-green feathers. Cut the 2 small oval logs into ⅛-inch slices, rolling out and reshaping as needed to keep the oval shape, to make 20 light green ovals and 10 darker green ovals. Roll out and shape the 3 reserved purple head feathers to keep the teardrop shape. Transfer the shapes to the pans. Cover the pans with plastic wrap to prevent drying.

4 Spoon 1 teaspoon vanilla frosting into a ziplock bag. Tint 2 teaspoons vanilla frosting yellow with the food coloring and spoon into a ziplock bag. Tint ¼ cup of vanilla frosting blue with the food coloring and spoon into a ziplock bag. Press the excess air from the bags and seal. Tint the remaining vanilla frosting green with the green and yellow food coloring.

5 Place the cake layer on a clean work surface. Starting at the bottom of the cake, trim 1¾ inches on the diagonal from each side (it will look like a fan; see diagram). Cut one trimmed piece in half crosswise. Transfer the cake to a large serving platter. Place the trimmed piece of cake on top of the fan shape, standing on its long side, with the pointed end 2 inches from the bottom of the fan, using the green frosting to secure it (this will be the support for the cookie head). Spread the top and sides of the cake and the cake support with some of the green frosting. Spread the remaining green frosting on top of the cupcakes and smooth. Arrange the cupcakes in 2 rows behind the untrimmed area of cake as the tail, 5 cupcakes closest to the cake and 6 in the outer row.

fan shape

head support

discard

discard

1¾-inch width

6 Starting on the outer row of cupcakes, arrange the candy clay feathers, alternating the double-green and spotted feathers on top of the cupcakes, pressing into the frosting to secure. Repeat with 2 more rows, this time all spotted feathers, each overlapping slightly on the previous row of cupcakes. Arrange the remaining plain feathers on the outer edge of cake, overlapping the cupcakes slightly. Add an overlapping row of the darker green ovals. Add 2 more rows of the light green ovals closest to the neck and head.

7 Snip a small (⅛-inch) corner from the 3 bags with the frostings. Place the S-shaped cookie at the bottom of the cake, leaning it against the cake support, as the head and neck of the peacock, adding some blue frosting to secure it. Pipe the remaining blue frosting on top of the cookie and spread to smooth. Pipe a dot of vanilla frosting for the eye. Pipe an outline of the eye with the yellow frosting and add the brown candy in the center. Press the cut end of the banana candy into the blue frosting as the beak. Insert the 3 chocolate-coated wheat sticks behind the top of the head into the cake. Pipe a dot of the remaining vanilla frosting at the tips of the sticks and add the remaining 3 purple feathers as the head feathers.

candy clay

Edible modeling clay made from morsels and light corn syrup takes color well and stays flexible. (See the recipe on page 230 for quantities and melting times.)

• **Place the morsels (white chocolate for tinting, or chocolate or butterscotch) in a microwavable glass bowl. Microwave on high, stopping to stir every 20 seconds, until just well blended, about 1 minute total (do not overheat).**

• **Add light corn syrup to the melted morsels and mix well. Cover with plastic wrap and let sit for at least 3 hours to firm.**

• **Knead the firm clay on a work surface until smooth. To tint, add food coloring and knead until the color is evenly blended.**

• **Roll out the clay to the desired thickness between sheets of waxed paper. If it becomes too firm to work at any point, return it to the microwave for a few seconds to soften.**

guys and dolls

You know what boys like. Boys like paparazzi camera brownies, skateboard rice cereal treats, and camouflage cakes with ducks. You know what girls want. Girls want cookie makeup, cookie dolls with candy clothes, and cupcake shoes. Boys like . . . girls like . . . sweets!

PAPARAZZI PARTY

MAKES 2 SNAPSHOT BROWNIES, 4 CAMERA BROWNIES, AND 4 FLASH BROWNIES; ABOUT 12 SERVINGS

Brownie cameras, celebrity snapshots, glamour, and pop: this party has it all. The black-and-white design is chic, yet really easy to make, using flooded frosting on brownie squares.

1½ **cups canned vanilla frosting**
   Black food coloring (McCormick)
1 **can (16 ounces) plus 1 cup dark chocolate frosting**
1 **recipe Perfect Brownie Mix (page 228), baked in a 9-by-13-inch pan**
8 **creme-filled chocolate sandwich cookies (Oreos)**
4 **white mint gum squares (Orbit)**
4 **black licorice pastels (Jelly Belly)**
4 **mini marshmallows**
4 **black licorice laces (see Sources)**

1 Tint ⅓ cup of the vanilla frosting gray with the black food coloring. Spoon the gray frosting into a ziplock bag. Spoon ½ cup of the vanilla frosting into each of two separate ziplock bags. Tint the dark chocolate frosting black with the food coloring. Spoon ½ cup of the black frosting into each of two separate ziplock bags. Press out the excess air and seal the bags.

2 Remove the whole brownie from the pan and trim the edges even. Spread the remaining black frosting on top and smooth. Refrigerate the frosted brownie until set, about 30 minutes.

3 Using a thin knife, cut a 3½-inch-wide strip from the long edge of the brownie. Cut the strip in half crosswise to make the 2 snapshot brownies. Cut the remaining brownie piece in half lengthwise to make two 2¼-inch-wide strips. Cut each of the remaining strips crosswise into two 2-inch pieces for the 4 pops and two 3½-inch pieces for the 4 cameras.

4 For the cameras, using a small knife, slice along the inside of one cookie half to separate it from the creme filling, leaving a creme-filled and a plain side. Discard the plain side. Snip a small (⅛-inch) corner from one of the bags with the black frosting. For the camera lens, pipe a dot of black frosting closer to the right side of one of the 4 medium brownies. Attach 1 whole cookie. Pipe a dot of frosting on top of the cookie and add 1 creme-filled half, creme side up. Pipe a curved line of black frosting on the creme as the shadow. Press a gum piece on the upper left corner of the brownie as the flash. Insert a licorice pastel into the flat end of a marshmallow for the button and attach to the right edge of the brownie with a dot of frosting. For the strap, cut 1 licorice lace into an 8-inch length and press each end on opposite sides of the top edge of the brownie. Repeat to make 4 cameras.

5 For the pops, use a toothpick to lightly score a starburst on top of one of the small brownies. Snip a small (⅛-inch) corner from one of the bags of vanilla frosting and pipe the outline of the starburst shape. Repeat with the remaining 3 small brownies. Working with the vanilla frosting, place the bag in a small microwavable bowl with the cut corner up to prevent leakage. Microwave, massaging the bag frequently, until it has the texture of lightly whipped cream, 5 to 7 seconds. Massage the bag again. Carefully squeeze some of the melted frosting inside the outline of a starburst, using a toothpick or small paintbrush to help the frosting get into the smaller areas (see page 95). Tap the table lightly to help smooth the frosting. Repeat with the remaining 3 small brownies. Refrigerate until set, about 20 minutes. Use the bag with the black frosting to pipe the word "POP" on top of the starbursts.

6 For the photos, use a toothpick to lightly score the outline of each image on the 2 large brownies using the templates (page 93). Pipe the outline of the faces and hands with the black frosting (details will be piped later). Working with the already melted vanilla frosting, reheat the frosting in the microwave for about 3 seconds. Massage the bag again. Carefully squeeze some of the melted frosting inside the outlines of the hand and face, using a toothpick or small paintbrush to help the frosting get into the smaller areas. Tap the table lightly to help smooth the frosting. Snip a small (⅛-inch) corner from the bag of gray frosting, microwave, and repeat the process with the gray frosting for the hair and shirt and then the black frosting for the glasses. Refrigerate until set, about 20 minutes.

7 Snip a small (⅛-inch) corner from the remaining bags of black and vanilla frostings. Pipe the face details with the black frosting, using the photo (page 90) as a guide to add the eyes, ears, noses, mouths, curls, and shirt details. Pipe an outline around the outer edge of the brownies with the vanilla frosting. Arrange the paparazzi brownies on a serving platter.

flooding

"Flooded" frosting is an easy way to create smooth fields of color or intricate designs on treats. Piped lines create a dam that holds melted frosting in place.

- **Frost the treat you are flooding and smooth out the frosting. Place a template on top of the frosting (or draw free-form) and use a toothpick to outline the design.**

- **Using the colors of frosting called for in the recipe, snip small corners from freezer-weight ziplock bags of frosting and pipe outlines around all the areas you will flood.**

- **Melt the frosting in the microwave, as directed in the recipe, and flood the areas within the piped outlines. Use a toothpick or small paintbrush to direct the frosting into small areas of the drawing.**

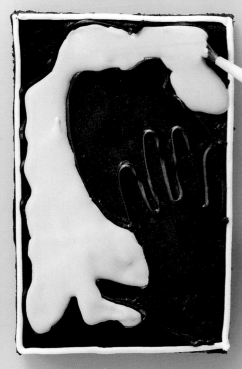

PAPER DOLL COOKIES

MAKES 16 COOKIE DOLLS; 8 PER RECIPE

Making designer fabric from Candy Clay is easy. Just roll it, cut it, combine it, and roll it again. To get a perfect fit, cut out clothes with the same cookie cutter used for the cookie. That way, there are no alterations needed.

2 recipes Quick Sugar Cookie Dough (page 226), any flavor
2 recipes Candy Clay (page 230), made with white chocolate
   Yellow, red, green, neon blue, purple, and black food coloring (see Sources)
½ recipe Candy Clay, made with semisweet chocolate chips
¼ recipe Candy Clay, made with butterscotch chips
1 recipe Royal Frosting (page 232)
   Thin ribbon

SUNBATHER
Chocolate, light green, yellow, and blue candy clay

LUMBERJACK
Chocolate, white, red, and gray candy clay
1 thin pretzel stick (Bachman)

CARMEN
Yellow, pink, and purple candy clay
Fruit-shaped hard candies

TIE GUY
Green and blue candy clay
Yellow candy decor (Cake Mate)

UNION SUIT
Yellow and red candy clay
Yellow candy decors (Cake Mate)
Mini bear-shaped graham cracker (Teddy Grahams)

CAVE WOMAN
Chocolate, butterscotch, and white candy clay
Thin honey wheat stick (Pringles)

CHEF
White, blue, and butterscotch candy clay
Marshmallow, halved lengthwise
White royal frosting
White candy decors (Cake Mate)
Black jelly bean, halved lengthwise

BAG LADY
Red, white, green, pink, and yellow candy clay
Red heart and green star decors (Cake Mate)
Green and pink fruit-shaped hard candies

1 Follow the directions for the Quick Sugar Cookie Dough through step 1. Cut out 16 cookies using 5-inch gingerbread boy or girl cookie cutters (see Sources). Transfer the shapes to the cookie sheets about 1 inch apart. Use a drinking straw to make a small hole in each hand for the ribbon. Continue with step 3 to bake the cookies. Cool on a wire rack.

2 Line three cookie sheets with waxed paper. Tint enough white chocolate candy clay into the desired colors to make the fabrics of your choice. Knead until well blended. Roll out one color of the clay at a time between 2 sheets of waxed paper to a ⅛-inch thickness. Using a fluted pastry wheel, a paring knife, small scissors, or cookie cutters, cut the rolled candy clay into shapes (see clay patterns, page 101). After assembling the patterns, use the same gingerbread boy or girl cookie cutter used for the cookies to trim the clay to fit. Transfer the clothing shapes to the cookie sheets. Repeat with the scraps and the other pieces of clay, keeping covered with plastic wrap to prevent drying. Shape the remaining candy clay scraps by hand, using candies for accents to make the accessories: suntan lotion bottle (chocolate and yellow clay), beach towel (neon blue and green candy clay, textured with a grater), ax (gray candy clay and thin pretzel stick), fruit hat and dress decoration and green shoes (fruit-shaped hard candies), tie tack, buttons, star, and lips (candy decors), teddy bear (Teddy Grahams), club (butterscotch candy clay and wheat stick), bone (white candy clay), chef's hat (marshmallow and white royal frosting), spoon (butterscotch candy clay), clogs (black jelly beans), hair barrette (pink candy clay), and purse (yellow candy clay and pink banana-shaped hard candy). Transfer the pieces to the cookie sheets.

3 Divide the royal frosting between two ziplock bags. Press out the excess air and seal the bags. Snip a very small (1/16-inch) corner from a bag. Pipe dots of frosting on the back side of the candy-clay cutouts. Attach the clay to the cookies. Pipe dots of frosting on top of the cookies to add the extra decorations. Let the cookies dry for at least 30 minutes.

4 Thread a thin ribbon through the holes in the hands to tie the cookies together.

a perfect fit

clay patterns

You can make vivid patterns in tinted clay "fabrics" for cookie dolls. Using the same cookie cutter that you used to make the cookie dolls, cut clothes from candy-clay fabrics to fit the cookies.

• Inlay patterns start with contrasting colors of clay. Using any shape cutter, remove shapes from the background color. Cut the same shapes from contrasting colors and insert in the open holes of the background. Roll lightly with a rolling pin to adhere.

• Rickrack fabrics can be made using a pastry wheel. Cut colorful strips from tinted clay. Overlap the strips to create fabric.

• Variegated patterns are made with two or three different colors of clay. White chocolate, butterscotch, and chocolate make a striking pattern. Roll the clay into thin logs and twist the logs together. Roll the twist flat to create random blended patterns. Use a small knife or cookie cutter to create the shapes for the clothes.

CRISPY SK8TER CAKE

NO-BAKE • MAKES 1 SKATEBOARD; ABOUT 24 SERVINGS

This skateboard gets its pop from the crispy marshmallow rice cereal treats that run from nose to tail. Underneath, it is reinforced with a coating of chocolate and cookie trucks. Finish the scene with your own sketchy skating course drawn with melted chocolate.

 1 recipe Chocolate Rice Cereal Treat (page 229)
 3½ recipes Rice Cereal Treats (page 229)
   Neon blue, yellow, and black food coloring (McCormick)
   Nonstick cooking spray
 4 yellow candy-coated chocolates (M&M's)
 2 bags (14 ounces each) plus 1 cup dark cocoa candy melting wafers (Wilton)
 17 chocolate-covered graham crackers (Keebler)
 7 anisette toasts (Stella D'oro)

1 Press the chocolate rice cereal treat firmly into a 21-by-1½-inch rectangle on parchment paper or waxed paper. Use a measuring cup coated with nonstick cooking spray to flatten the sides and top of the treat.

2 Tint 1 recipe of the plain rice cereal treat neon blue with the food coloring. Press the blue treat around the chocolate rectangle, about 1¼ inches wide on either side of the chocolate treat, tapering it at one end. Use the measuring cup and a ruler coated with nonstick cooking spray to help flatten the top and sides of the treat, pressing firmly.

3 Tint 2 recipes of the rice cereal treats yellow with the food coloring. Press the yellow treat around the other treats, about 1¾ inches wide on either side of the blue treat, tapering it around the tapered blue end and rounding the opposite end. Use the measuring cup to help flatten the treat skateboard, pressing very firmly.

4 For the wheels, tint the remaining ½ recipe of rice cereal treat gray with the black food coloring. Grease your hands and the inside of a ½-cup dry measuring cup with nonstick cooking spray. Divide the gray treat into quarters. Firmly press one quarter of the mixture into the cup and flatten the top. Unmold and repeat to make 3 more wheels. Press a yellow chocolate in the center of each. Allow the skateboard and wheels to rest for at least 2 hours before handling again.

5 Place the skateboard on the back of a large cookie sheet, the side with the best-looking stripes down. Place 1 cup of the candy melts in a ziplock bag. Do not seal the bag. Microwave the remaining candy melts in a bowl, stopping to stir frequently, until smooth, about 1½ minutes. Spread the melted candy in an even layer on the skateboard, making sure to spread the candy right up to the edges.

truck

support

deck

truck

6 Microwave the candy melts in the ziplock bag for 10 seconds to soften. Massage the candy, return to the microwave, and repeat the process until the candy is smooth, about 1 minute. Press out the excess air and seal the bag. Snip a small (⅛-inch) corner from the bag. Pipe a generous dot of the candy about 3½ inches in from each short end of the board and press 2 chocolate graham crackers, side by side and flat side down, into the melted candy at each end. Pipe more candy in 3 spots lengthwise down the center of the board and add 3 more graham crackers, flat side down. Refrigerate until set, about 30 minutes.

7 To make the trucks, line a cookie sheet with waxed paper. Using a serrated knife, trim a 1-inch piece from one short end of 4 of the anisette toasts (see photo). Pipe some of the melted candy on each trimmed end of the toasts. Press the 2 ends together to make a long cookie. Repeat to make another long cookie. Transfer to the cookie sheet, flat side down, and refrigerate until set, 5 minutes.

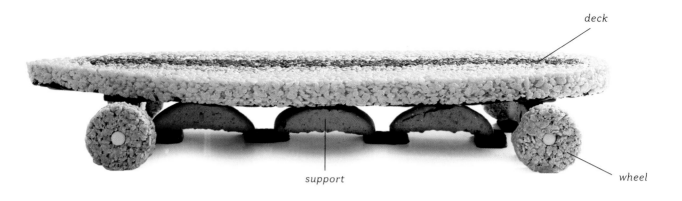

deck

support *wheel*

8 For the skateboard supports, place the remaining 10 graham crackers on the cookie sheet, flat side down. Pipe a generous dot of melted candy on top of each graham cracker. Arrange each end of an anisette toast, rounded side up, on the melted candy on one of the graham crackers to give each toast two feet for support. Repeat with the remaining toasts and graham crackers, including the 2 longer toasts, and refrigerate until set, 5 minutes.

9 If the candy becomes too firm to pipe, reheat in the microwave for 5 to 10 seconds, massaging the bag, until smooth. Pipe generous dots of melted candy on top of the cookies attached to the board. Add the 2 long anisette toasts with cookie feet, crosswise and cookie feet up, at each short end of the board and the 3 smaller toasts, lengthwise and cookie feet up, down the center of the board (see photo). Let stand until set, about 20 minutes.

10 Invert the skateboard on a serving platter or cardboard surface. Pipe a dot of the melted candy on the outside edge of the outer toasts. Add a wheel, yellow candy facing out, and press to secure. Repeat with the remaining wheels. Pipe lines and squiggles on the serving surface with the remaining melted candy.

crispy treat

Rice cereal treats can be made in any shape and tinted for extra pizzazz.

- Place the marshmallows and butter (see the recipe, page 229) in a bowl and microwave until melted, about 1½ minutes. Stir until smooth.

- Add the food coloring and mix to blend the color.

- Fold the rice cereal into the mixture until it is well blended.

- Coat your hands with nonstick cooking spray and form the treat according to the recipe. Use a smooth tool to shape and flatten the treat.

MY CUPCAKE PAGE

MAKES 1 SOCIAL NETWORK; ABOUT 24 SERVINGS

If your social network is all about cupcakes, then you'll want a computer tablet made from a crispy marshmallow rice cereal treat with a sheet-cake screen. Add a personalized bio to create a fabulous birthday surprise.

- 20 yellow, 8 white, 8 purple, 8 orange, 6 green spice drops, and 1 red spice drop
- ½ cup yellow decorating sugar (Cake Mate)
- ¼ cup each light pink, purple, orange, and green decorating sugar (see Sources)
- 1 tablespoon red decorating sugar (Cake Mate)
- ¼ cup dark chocolate frosting
- ¼ cup milk chocolate frosting
- 1 can (16 ounces) plus ½ cup vanilla frosting
  Red and yellow food coloring
- 1 recipe Perfect Cake Mix (page 224), made with yellow cake and baked in a 9-by-13-inch pan
- 2 recipes Chocolate Rice Cereal Treat (page 229)
- 6 mini chocolate peanut butter cups (Reese's Minis)
- 1 chocolate mini muffin or mini cupcake
- 4 white chocolate candies (Hershey's Cookies'n'Creme Drops)
- 3 chocolate peanut butter cups (Reese's)
- 2 teaspoons multicolored nonpareil sprinkles
- 2 teaspoons multicolored decors
- 1 tablespoon mini candy-coated chocolates (M&M's Minis)

1 For the colorful candy areas, press like-colored spice drops together. Roll out each color of spice drop on a work surface sprinkled with the same color sugar to a ⅛-inch thickness (roll the white spice drops in the light pink sugar). Cut an 8½-by-3-inch rectangle and a 1½-inch oval from the yellow spice drops, a 2½-by-3-inch rectangle from the pink spice drops, a 2½-inch square from the orange spice drops, three 1-by-2¼-inch rectangles from the green spice drops, a 1½-by-4½-inch rectangle from the purple spice drops, and a ¾-inch heart from the red spice drop, rerolling the scraps as necessary.

2 Spoon the dark chocolate and the milk chocolate frostings into separate ziplock bags. Tint ¼ cup of the vanilla frosting pink with the red food coloring and spoon into a ziplock bag. Spoon 1 cup of the vanilla frosting into a ziplock bag. Press out the excess air and seal the bags. Tint the remaining vanilla frosting a pale yellow with the food coloring.

3 Trim the top of the cake level with a serrated knife. Transfer the cake, trimmed side down, to a serving platter (the bottom side of the cake is flatter). Spread the pale yellow frosting over the top and sides of the cake and smooth (don't worry if the frosting on the sides seems thin; this will be covered with the chocolate rice cereal treat).

4 Shape and press the chocolate rice cereal treat around the outside of a 9-by-13-inch cake pan, making it about 2 inches wide on one short side of the pan and 1 inch wide on the remaining sides, pressing firmly. Make a cut in one narrow side of the treat and lift it from around the pan (see photo). Transfer it to the platter and wrap it around the frosted cake, sealing the opening by pressing the edges back together.

5 Place the flattened spice drop pieces on top of the cake (see photo, page 109, for arrangement).

6 Cut the mini peanut butter cups in half from top to bottom. Using a serrated knife, cut the mini chocolate muffin in half, keeping the paper liner intact around the muffin halves. Snip a small (⅛-inch) corner from the bags with the dark chocolate, vanilla, and pink frostings. Snip a very small (1⁄16-inch) corner from the bag with the milk chocolate frosting. Pipe "My Cupcake Page" on top of the yellow spice drop rectangle with the dark chocolate frosting. Pipe an outline with the vanilla frosting around the edge of the cake and the edge of the yellow spice drop rectangle. Attach the white chocolate candies and the yellow oval on the wider edge of the cereal treat with some of the vanilla frosting. Pipe headings under or on top of the flattened spice drop pieces on the cake with the milk chocolate frosting. Pipe swirls of the milk chocolate, pink, and vanilla frostings on top of the whole large and halved mini peanut butter cups. Add some sprinkles to the halved mini peanut butter cups and place them, cut side down, on the cake. Arrange the 3 whole peanut butter cups on top of the purple spice drop rectangle; attach with dots of frosting. Pipe the pink frosting on top of one of the muffin halves. Top the muffin with the decors and place on top of the pink spice drop rectangle along with more decors, attaching with dots of frosting. Add the mini chocolates on top of the orange spice drop square; attach with dots of frosting.

HIGH HEEL CUPCAKES

MAKES 12 PAIRS; 24 CUPCAKES

These cupcakes are made for walking! Start with cupcakes baked in fashionable paper liners, add chocolate-coated soles and wafer-cookie heels, and finish with fashion-forward sugar colors for a look that will set you back on your heels.

BASIC SHOE METHOD

- 12 **graham crackers**
- 12 **vanilla or chocolate cookie sticks (Pirouettes, Oreo Fun Stix)**
- 1½ **cups white or cocoa candy melting wafers (Wilton)**
- 1 **cup decorating sugar, color-coordinated to match shoe style (see Sources)**
- 2 **cans (16 ounces each) vanilla frosting**
  Food coloring, color-coordinated to match shoe style
- 24 **cupcakes baked in liner style of your choice, 2 cupcakes per style**

1 For the soles, place a graham cracker on a work surface. Using a small serrated knife with a back and forth sawing motion, cut the graham cracker in half crosswise. Remove a corner, angled to ¾ inch, on both sides of each cracker half to make the tapered sole (see photo). Repeat with the remaining graham crackers. Cut the cookie sticks in half crosswise into two 2¾-inch lengths. Cut one end at an angle.

2 Line a cookie sheet with waxed paper. Place the candy melting wafers in a glass bowl. Microwave for 10 seconds, stir, and repeat until the candies are melted and smooth, about 1 minute. Dip the cut crackers into the melted candy, one at a time, to cover, allowing the excess candy to drip back into the bowl, and smooth with an offset spatula. Transfer the coated cracker to the cookie sheet. Repeat with the remaining crackers and candy. Refrigerate until set, about 5 minutes. Save the excess candy melts to attach the heels.

3 Place the decorating sugar (use the color to match the shoe style) in a shallow bowl. Spoon ½ cup of the vanilla frosting into a ziplock bag. Tint the remaining vanilla frosting with the food coloring (use the color to match the shoe style). Spoon ½ cup of the tinted frosting into a ziplock bag. Press out the excess air and seal the bags. Spread the remaining tinted frosting on top of the cupcakes, mounding it slightly. Roll the tops of the cupcakes in the decorating sugar to cover completely. Refrigerate the cup-

cakes for about 15 minutes. Using a 2-inch round cookie cutter or the rim of a glass, mark a 1-inch-deep semicircle from the edge of a sugared cupcake (see photo). Remove the semicircle of cake and frosting with a small knife. For open-toed shoes, make a ½-inch semicircle cut on the opposite side of the cupcake from the first cut. Repeat with the remaining cupcakes. Snip a small (⅛-inch) corner from the bags with the vanilla and tinted frostings. Pipe vanilla frosting over the exposed cake in the cut areas.

4 Carefully peel the candy-coated crackers from the waxed paper. Trim any uneven edges with a small knife. Pipe a line of tinted frosting around the 2 long sides and 1 short side of each cracker. Dip the frosted edges into the decorating sugar to coat.

5 Reheat the reserved candy melts in the microwave for 5 to 10 seconds to soften. Stir the candy, return to the microwave, and repeat the process until the candy is smooth, about 30 seconds. Dip one angled end of a cookie stick into the melted candy. Working on one shoe at a time on a small serving plate, press the large end of the cracker sole into the cut area (2-inch semicircle) of the cupcake, candy side up. For the heel, place the cookie stick, dipped end up to secure, under the small end of the sole. Repeat with the remaining cupcakes, crackers, and cookies. Allow to set for at least 20 minutes.

TO ACCESSORIZE THE SHOES

To make the shoes even more fashionable, you will need frosting and a selection of candies and gums of your choice. Candy decors (Cake Mate, Wilton, Red Hots), candy-coated chocolates (M&M's Minis, Sixlets), gum balls, small hard candies, pearlized candies (SweetWorks), and gum for bows can all be used for shoe accents. Use frosting to attach decorations and pipe outlines along the cut edges of the cupcakes.

TO MAKE BOWS Cut a 1¾-inch length from a stick of gum. Cut the remaining small piece in half lengthwise. Pinch the center of the long piece of gum. Wrap one of the smaller pieces around the pinched area to finish the bow.

TO MAKE SWIRL PATTERNS Spoon vanilla frosting into a ziplock bag. Press out the excess air and seal the bag. Cut a small (⅛-inch) corner from the bag and pipe swirled lines of vanilla frosting on top of the sugared cupcakes.

TO MAKE ZEBRA PRINT Spoon dark chocolate frosting into a ziplock bag. Press out the excess air and seal the bag. Snip a small (⅛-inch) corner from the bag. Following the basic method above, pipe wavy lines of dark chocolate frosting on top of the vanilla-frosted cupcake before rolling it in white sugar (see photo).

DUCK BLIND

MAKES 1 DUCK BLIND AND ABOUT 12 DUCKS; ABOUT 10 SERVINGS

Looks like camo patterns are in season, and now they're on dessert, too, thanks to a fun technique called flooding. Just pipe a color outline with frosting, melt some frosting to liquefy, and flood inside the outline. That's camo-licious!

To make a pretty pattern for girls, use pink and chocolate frosting (see photo, page 119).

DUCKS AND CATTAILS
1 recipe Quick Spice Cookie Dough (page 227)
All-purpose flour
¾ cup canned vanilla frosting
Green food coloring
¼ cup green decorating sugar (Cake Mate)
12 mini chocolate chips (Nestlé)
6 thin honey wheat sticks (Pringles)
3 chocolate chews (Tootsie Rolls)
¼ cup granulated sugar, plus more if needed
6 candy spearmint leaves (Farley's)

CAMO CAKE
1 can (16 ounces) milk chocolate frosting
1 can (16 ounces) vanilla frosting
Green and yellow food coloring
1 9-inch round chocolate cake layer (Perfect Cake Mix, page 224)

1 **DUCKS:** Preheat the oven to 350°F. Line two cookie sheets with parchment paper.

2 Roll out the spice cookie dough on a lightly floured surface to a scant ¼-inch thickness. Using a small paring knife and the duck template, cut the rolled-out dough into about 12 duck shapes, cutting as closely as possible and rerolling the scraps as necessary. Transfer the cutouts to the cookie sheets, about 1 inch apart. Bake the cookies until firm to the touch and lightly golden, 10 to 12 minutes. Transfer to a wire rack and cool completely.

3 Spoon ¼ cup of the vanilla frosting into a ziplock bag. Press out the excess air and seal the bag. Tint the remaining frosting green with the food coloring. Microwave the green frosting in a small bowl, stopping to stir frequently, until it has the texture of lightly whipped cream, 5 to 10 seconds. Holding a duck cookie by the body, spoon a small amount of the melted frosting over the duck head area, making sure not to cover the beak and allowing the excess frosting

to drip back into the bowl. Sprinkle the frosted area with the green sugar to cover completely. Transfer the cookie to a wire rack. Repeat with the remaining cookies.

4 For the eyes, press a mini chocolate chip, pointed end down, into the frosting. Snip a small (⅛-inch) corner from the bag with the vanilla frosting. For the neck, pipe a line of frosting at the base of the green frosting. Repeat with the remaining cookies.

5 **CATTAILS:** For the cattails, cut the wheat sticks in half crosswise. Microwave the chocolate chews for no more than 3 seconds to soften. Quarter the chocolate chews and flatten each piece slightly into a small rectangle. Wrap 1 chocolate chew around the top of each wheat stick, leaving ¼ inch of the stick showing, pressing gently to secure (the wheat sticks are fragile).

6 For the reeds, sprinkle the granulated sugar on a work surface. Roll out the spearmint leaves to a scant ¼-inch thickness, using additional sugar as necessary to prevent sticking. Cut the flattened candies into twelve 1¼-inch zigzag reed shapes with scissors.

7 **CAMO CAKE:** Spoon ½ cup of the milk chocolate frosting into a small bowl. Stir in 1 tablespoon of the vanilla frosting to make a lighter brown. Spoon the frosting into a ziplock bag. Divide the remaining vanilla frosting among 3 bowls. Tint each bowl a different shade of green with the green and yellow food coloring. Spoon each color frosting into a separate ziplock bag. Press out the excess air and seal the bags.

8 Trim the top of the cake level with a serrated knife. Place the cake, cut side down (the bottom of the cake is flatter), on a 12-inch serving platter with a lip. Spread the remaining chocolate frosting on the sides and a thin layer on top of the cake and smooth.

9 Snip a small (⅛-inch) corner from all the bags of frosting. Pipe outlines of 2- to 3-inch camouflage shapes on the top of the cake with the different colors of frostings. Make sure the lines of tinted frosting butt up against one another (see photo).

10 Working with one tinted frosting at a time, place a bag of the frosting in a small microwavable bowl, with the cut corner up to prevent leakage. Microwave, massaging the bag frequently, until it has the texture of lightly whipped cream, 3 to 5 seconds. Massage the bag again. Carefully squeeze some of the melted frosting inside the same-color outline. Use a toothpick or small paintbrush to help the frosting get into the small areas. Tap the platter lightly to help smooth the frosting. Repeat with the remaining frosting and outlines.

11 Arrange the duck cookies, wheat stick cattails, and spearmint reeds all around the side of the cake, using the lip of the platter for support. Serve the additional cookies alongside.

camo-flooding

This simple technique makes piping camouflage patterns a cinch.

• Tint the frostings and place in ziplock bags.

• Pipe outlines in each color. Be sure the lines touch.

• Melt the frosting in the microwave and flood the outlines with the same-color frosting. Use a toothpick to nudge the frosting into smaller areas.

IN THE BAG

MAKES 12 HANDBAGS

Get carried away with bags so big, they hold two cupcakes, frosting, licorice twists, and candy for stylish bling.

 1 **can (16 ounces) dark chocolate frosting**
   Black and neon pink food coloring (McCormick)
 1 **can (16 ounces) vanilla frosting**
 1 **can (16 ounces) milk chocolate frosting**
 8 **vanilla cupcakes baked in black paper liners (see Sources)**
 8 **vanilla cupcakes baked in gold foil liners (see Sources)**
 8 **vanilla cupcakes baked in pink foil liners (Reynolds)**
 2 **black licorice twists (Red Vines Black Licorice)**
 2 **chocolate licorice twists (Chocolate Twizzlers)**
 3 **pink licorice twists (Rainbow Twizzlers)**
12 **thin pretzel sticks (Bachman)**
 3 **yellow fruit chews (Laffy Taffy, Starburst)**
 4 **yellow candy-coated chocolates (M&M's)**
   Gold shimmer dust (Wilton)
 8 **large gold dragées or yellow candy pearls (see Sources)**
12 **chocolate chews (Tootsie Rolls)**
 1 **tablespoon gold dragées or yellow pearl sprinkles (Wilton)**
 2 **teaspoons pink candy pearls (Wilton)**

1 Tint the dark chocolate frosting black with the food coloring. Spoon ⅓ cup of the black frosting into a ziplock bag. Tint the vanilla frosting light pink with the food coloring. Spoon ¼ cup of the pink frosting into a ziplock bag. Spoon ¼ cup of the milk chocolate frosting into a ziplock bag. Press out the excess air and seal the bags.

2 Trim the tops of the cupcakes level with a serrated knife. Remove the liners from 4 of each color, keeping the best-looking of each intact. Spread some of the remaining frosting on top of the cupcakes with the liners: black for black liners, milk chocolate for gold liners, and pink for pink liners. Place an unwrapped cupcake, trimmed side down, on top of a frosted cupcake, pressing down to secure. Trim a ¾-inch corner from each side of the top cupcake (see photo, page 54). Repeat with the remaining cupcakes. Freeze until firm, about 20 minutes.

3 Spread a thin layer of matching-color frosting over the frozen cupcakes and smooth. Return the cupcakes to the freezer until ready to dip.

4 Tint the remaining light pink frosting (not the frosting in the ziplock bag) bright pink with additional food coloring. Microwave the bright pink frosting in a glass measuring cup, stopping to stir frequently, until it has the texture of lightly whipped cream, 20 to 30 seconds. Holding a chilled pink cupcake by the liner, dip it into the melted frosting up to the liner, allowing the excess frosting to drip back into the cup. Turn right side up, tap the bottom of the cupcake lightly to flatten the frosting, and let stand. If the melted frosting begins to thicken, reheat it in the microwave for several seconds, stirring well. Repeat with the remaining cupcakes and frosting colors to make 4 of each color.

5 For the handles, cut ¼ inch from each end of the black, chocolate, and pink licorice twists. Cut 2 twists of each color in half crosswise. Cut the pretzel sticks in half crosswise. Insert a pretzel stick, about ½ inch in, at each end of the cut twists.

6 To make the decorations, line a cookie sheet with waxed paper. For the tassels, cut the remaining pink licorice twist into four 1½-inch pieces. Use a small knife to make thin lengthwise cuts, about 1¼ inches deep, on each tassel piece. Transfer the tassels to the cookie sheet. For the yellow flowers, microwave the yellow fruit chews for no more than 3 seconds to soften. Press the fruit chews together and roll out on a work surface into a 4-inch oval. Cut four 1-inch flower shapes from the fruit chew with a small cookie cutter (see Sources) or scissors and place them on the cookie sheet. Press a yellow candy into the center of each flower. Using a small paintbrush, brush the flower with some of the gold dust. For the chocolate bows, microwave the chocolate chews for no more than 3 seconds to soften. Press 3 chocolate chews together and roll out on a work surface into a 3½-inch square. Repeat with the remaining chocolate chews. Cut each square into one 2½-by-1-inch rectangle, two 2-by-1-inch rectangles, and one 1-by-½-inch rectangle. Pinch the center of the larger rectangle together. Wrap the smallest rectangle lengthwise around the pinched area to create the bow. Cut a notch from a short end of each of the 2 remaining rectangles and pinch the opposite end for the tails. Arrange the bow shape on the cookie sheet, pressing lightly to secure the pieces. Brush the bow with the gold dust.

7 To assemble the black purses, snip a small (⅛-inch) corner from the bag with the black frosting. Pipe diagonal lines of frosting in a lattice pattern, about ½ inch apart, over an entire cupcake. Press a fruit chew flower on one trimmed side of the cupcake. For the handle, insert the 2 pretzel ends with the black licorice twist at the top of the cupcake about 1½ inches apart. Place 2 large gold dragées under the handle as the clasp. Repeat with the remaining black cupcakes.

8 To assemble the brown purses, sprinkle the brown-frosted cupcakes with the gold dust to coat. Snip a small (⅛-inch) corner from the bag with the milk chocolate frosting. Pipe 3 dots of frosting close together in a regular pattern over one of the cupcakes. Use tweezers to attach the small gold dragées in the center of each dot of frosting. For the handle, insert the 2 pretzel ends with the chocolate licorice twist at the top of the cupcake about 1½ inches apart. Attach a chocolate bow on one trimmed side of the cupcake with a dot of frosting. Repeat with the remaining brown cupcakes.

9 To assemble the pink purses, snip a small (⅛-inch) corner from the bag with the light pink frosting. Pipe short lines of frosting to look like stitching around the bottom, up the sides, and in a V shape on one trimmed side of one of the cupcakes. For the handle, insert the 2 pretzel ends with the pink licorice twist at the top of the cupcake about 1½ inches apart. Press a pink licorice tassel, fringe side down, at the base of the V with a dot of frosting to secure. Pipe several dots of frosting on and near the licorice handle and at the base of the V stitching and add the pink candy pearls. Repeat with the remaining pink cupcakes.

DARTBOARD

MAKES ONE 10-INCH TARGET, ABOUT 16 SERVINGS

Aiming to please? Target some fun with a brownie dartboard decorated with flooded frosting and darts assembled from spice drops and pretzels. It's easier than it looks and hits the bull's-eye every time.

BOARD
1 can (16 ounces) vanilla frosting
  Black, red, and green food coloring (McCormick)
1 can (16 ounces) dark chocolate frosting
1 recipe Perfect Brownie Mix (page 228), baked in a 10-inch round pan (see Sources)

DARTS
2 rolls (0.75 ounce each) strawberry fruit leather (Fruit by the Foot)
3 each large red, black, green, and yellow spice drops
3 each red and green spice drops
6 thin pretzel sticks (Bachman)

1 **BOARD:** Divide the vanilla frosting among 4 small bowls. Tint one bowl light gray with a drop of the black food coloring, one bowl red, and one bowl green, leaving one bowl white. Spoon each color frosting into a separate ziplock bag. Tint ¾ cup of the dark chocolate frosting black with the food coloring and spoon it into a ziplock bag. Press out the excess air and seal the bags.

2 Place the brownie, top side down, on a flat serving platter (the bottom of the brownie is flatter). Spread the remaining dark chocolate frosting on the sides and a thin layer on top of the brownie and smooth.

3 Cut out 8-inch, 7½-inch, 4½-inch, 4-inch, 1¾-inch, and 1-inch circles from waxed paper. Center the largest circle on top of the brownie. Score lightly with a toothpick to mark an outline of the circle in the frosting. Repeat with the remaining circles to mark the rings of the dartboard. Use a ruler, toothpicks, and a thin knife to score 20 evenly spaced lines radiating from the 1¾-inch circle to the outer circle (they will be about 1⅛ inches apart where they meet the outside circle).

4 Snip a small (⅛-inch) corner from each of the bags with the frosting. Using the gray frosting, pipe an outline along the outer rim of the board and along all of the scored circles and lines. Working with the black frosting, place the bag of frosting in a small bowl, cut corner up to prevent leakage. Microwave, massaging the bag frequently, until it has the texture of lightly whipped cream, 10 to 15 seconds. Massage the bag again. Carefully squeeze some

of the melted black frosting in the outer ring (the area that will be behind the numbers). Fill the entire outer ring, using a toothpick or small paintbrush to help the frosting get into the small areas, and tap the platter lightly to help smooth the frosting. Pipe alternating openings of every other ray with the black frosting, using the photo as a guide for placement. Repeat with the white, green, and red frostings, melting one color at a time for 10 to 15 seconds and following the photo for placement. Refrigerate until set, about 20 minutes.

5 Pipe the numbers around the outer edge of the board using the gray frosting. Pipe small accent lines at the tip of each radiating line in the outer ring and on top of the small red and green inner circles to reinforce the look of the traditional metal wire design.

6 **DARTS:** For the feathers, unroll the fruit leather. Press each strip together, shiny side in, to make a double thickness. Cut the strips into twelve 2¼-inch-long pieces. Round the top of one short end and taper the opposite end of each piece with scissors. Make a 1½-inch lengthwise cut from the center of the rounded side of 6 of the fruit leather pieces. Make a 1½-inch cut from the center of the tapered end of the remaining 6 pieces. Slide 2 pieces with opposite cuts together to make the feather (see photo).

7 Cut a thin slice from the flat side of each large spice drop. Press the cut sides together to secure, black with red, and yellow with green. Trim a thin slice from the rounded ends of the black and yellow spice drops.

8 Cut a small X on the rounded side of each of the smaller spice drops and cut a thin slice from the flat side. Press the cut flat sides of the coordinating spice drops to the trimmed sides of the larger spice drops. Attach the feathers to the darts by inserting the tapered ends of the fruit leather into the X on top of the spice drops (see photo).

9 Insert a thin pretzel stick into the rounded end of each of the large spice drops. Arrange the candy darts around and on top of the dartboard brownie (if sticking the darts into the brownie, add just before serving).

COOKIE MAKEUP PARTY

NO-BAKE • MAKES 36 COSMETICS

You'll blush when your friends tell you how great these cookie compacts make you look. The foundation is store-bought chocolate cookies adorned with colorful candies. Add fruit chews and bubble gum, and you'll be sitting pretty.

Chocolate chews, soft caramels, or fruit chews (whichever is called for in each makeup project)
1 cup dark cocoa candy melting wafers (Wilton)

1 Line two cookie sheets with waxed paper. Microwave the chews or caramels for no more than 3 seconds to soften. Roll out on a work surface to a ⅛-inch thickness. Transfer to the cookie sheets.

2 Place the dark cocoa candy melting wafers in a ziplock bag (do not seal the bag). Microwave for 10 seconds to soften. Massage the wafers in the bag, return to the microwave, and repeat the process until the candy is smooth, about 50 seconds. Press out the excess air and seal the bag. When ready to start assembling the makeup, snip a small (⅛-inch) corner from the bag with the melted candy and follow the instructions for each project.

COMPACTS
10 fudge graham cookies (Rippin' Good)
5 assorted colored gum squares
10 soft caramels (Kraft), flattened (see above)

BLUSH
10 fudge mint cookies (Keebler Grasshopper)
5 mini candy-coated chocolates (M&M's Minis)
10 red fruit chews (Jolly Rancher), flattened

1 Pipe a dot of melted candy on the tops of 5 of each type of cookie. Add a piece of gum (compact) or a candy-coated chocolate (blush) to the dot and refrigerate until set, about 5 minutes.

2 Cut the flattened caramels into 2-inch squares. Trim ¼ inch from each corner. Cut the red fruit chews into 1¼-inch circles. Turn the remaining cookies flat side up, pipe a dot of melted candy on each, and add the appropriate flattened candy shape. Pipe a line of melted candy along one edge of each upturned cookie and place a matching chilled cookie, flat side down, on top. Line up the edges of the cookies and place the handle of a wooden spoon or a chopstick between the cookies to hold them open slightly until set, about 5 minutes.

MAKEUP PADS
2 tablespoons cornstarch
10 marshmallows

Dust the work surface with some of the cornstarch. Place a marshmallow on the surface, flat side down, and flatten with a rolling pin. Roll out to a 2-inch circle. Repeat with the remaining 9 marshmallows, dusting with more cornstarch as needed.

BRUSHES
6 chocolate chews (Tootsie Rolls), rolled out ⅛ inch thick
3 fudge stick cookies (Keebler)
2 green fruit chews (Laffy Taffy), rolled out ⅛ inch thick

1 Cut the rolled chocolate chews into six 1½-by-3-inch rectangles. Use scissors to cut each rectangle crosswise almost all the way to the top every scant ⅛ inch; it will look like a fringe. Roll up the chews along the uncut edge to form the bristles.

2 Cut a 1-inch piece from each end of the fudge sticks (discard the small scrap from the middle). Cut the rolled green fruit chews into six ¼-by-3-inch strips. Wrap a green fruit chew strip around the cookie along the cut edge, pressing to secure. Pipe some of the melted candy on the cut end of the cookie and attach a set of chocolate chew bristles. Repeat with the remaining cookies. Refrigerate until set, about 5 minutes.

LIPSTICK
5 chocolate-dipped wafer roll cookies (Bahlsen)
2 yellow fruit chews (Laffy Taffy), rolled out ⅛ inch thick
5 pink fruit chews (Laffy Taffy), *not* flattened

Trim ¾ inch from the plain end of the cookie wafers with a serrated knife. (You'll be using the chocolate end.) Cut the rolled yellow fruit chews into five ½-by-2½-inch strips. Wrap the fruit chew strips around the chocolate wafers at the cut edge and press to seal. For the lipstick, trim and shape each pink fruit chew into a ¾-inch log, about 1¾ inches long, with a tapered end. Pipe some melted candy at the cut end of the wafers and attach the flat end of the pink fruit chews. Refrigerate until set, about 5 minutes.

MASCARA

5 dark chocolate–coated wheat sticks (Pocky)

2 tablespoons chocolate sprinkles

5 fudge stick cookies (Keebler)

2 blue fruit chews (Jolly Rancher), rolled out ⅛ inch thick

1 Cut a 2½-inch piece from the chocolate end of each wheat stick. Pipe some melted candy on one end of each stick. While the candy is still wet, dip the end into the chocolate sprinkles to coat (see photo, page 51).

2 Cut ½ inch from one short end of each fudge stick. Cut the rolled blue fruit chews into five ⅓-by-3-inch strips. Wrap a fruit chew strip around the cut end of each fudge cookie, pressing to secure. Pipe some of the melted candy on the cut end of the cookies and attach the chocolate sticks. Refrigerate until set, about 5 minutes.

EYE SHADOW

3 mini marshmallows

2 dark chocolate–coated wheat sticks (Pocky)

6 chocolate-covered graham crackers (Keebler)

18 assorted pink and red gum squares

1 Cut the marshmallows in half crosswise. Cut a 1½-inch piece from the chocolate end of each wheat stick. Pipe a dot of melted candy on the cut ends of the wheat sticks. Place a cut marshmallow, flat side against the stick, into one end of the stick and let set, about 5 minutes.

2 Pipe 3 dots of melted candy in a line along one long edge on the flat side of each graham cracker and attach 3 different colors of gum. Refrigerate for 5 minutes, or until set.

BUMPER CAR SUNDAES

NO-BAKE • SERVES 12 SUNDAE DRIVERS

Dessert shells coated in colorful melted frosting and decorated with cookie wheels and eyes are ready to take your favorite ice cream and fixings for a rocky sundae drive.

- 12 **assorted colored spice drops**
- 12 **dark chocolate–coated wheat sticks (Pocky)**
- ½ **cup dark chocolate frosting**
- 2 **cans (16 ounces each) vanilla frosting**
  - **Red, yellow, green, and neon blue food coloring (McCormick)**
- 2 **packages (5 ounces each) dessert shell cakes (12 shells)**
- 60 **mini creme-filled chocolate sandwich cookies (Mini Oreos)**
- 24 **brown and 12 red mini candy-coated chocolates (M&M's Minis)**
- 12 **small scoops (1 quart) ice cream (vanilla or your favorite flavor)**
- ½ **cup hot fudge sauce**
- 2 **tablespoons mini candy decors (Cake Mate)**

1 For the flags, place a spice drop, flat side down, on a work surface. Trim ¼ inch from top to bottom on 2 opposite sides to leave a thin center slice. Trim the short straight side to expose the gummy interior and pinch the narrow end to make a triangle. Press the cut straight edge to the tip of a wheat stick. Repeat with the remaining spice drops and wheat sticks.

2 Spoon the chocolate frosting and ¼ cup of the vanilla frosting into separate ziplock bags. Press out the excess air and seal the bags. Divide the remaining vanilla frosting among 5 microwavable bowls. Tint each bowl a different bright color of orange (using red and yellow), yellow, red, neon blue, and green with the food coloring. Cover the bowls until ready to use to prevent drying.

3 Line two cookie sheets with waxed paper and place wire racks on top. Working with one color at a time, microwave a bowl of frosting, stirring every 5 seconds, until it has the texture of lightly whipped cream, 10 to 15 seconds. Use a spoon to coat a dessert shell with the melted frosting, covering the rim and the sides, allowing the excess frosting to drip back into the bowl. Transfer the dessert shell to a wire rack. Continue with the remaining dessert shells and frosting colors, making 3 shells of 2 colors and 2 shells of 3 colors. Refrigerate until set, about 20 minutes.

4 For the eyes, scrape the filling off 12 of the cookies. Snip a small (⅛-inch) corner from the bags with the vanilla and chocolate frostings. Pipe some vanilla frosting on the flat side of each of the 24 cookie halves and attach brown candies as the pupils.

5 Transfer each shell to a small serving plate. For the wheels, pipe 4 dots of chocolate frosting around the base of each dessert shell and attach a whole cookie to each. Using dots of chocolate frosting, attach the cookie eyes on one edge of the shell and add a red candy for the nose. Pipe lines of chocolate frosting on top of the cookie eyes to give expressions or use the squeeze-release-pull technique (see page 75) to create eyelashes. (The shells can be made up to this point and refrigerated for up to 3 hours.)

6 When ready to serve, add a scoop of ice cream to the well of each shell. Top with hot fudge sauce and some decors and insert a cookie flag at the back.

life of the party

Reinvent the party cake! Put it on a fork, and you've got piece-of-cake pops or puppy-love pops. Bake it in a measuring cup for an octopus's garden with oysters and jellyfish, or give it a girdle to make popover shakes from the soda shop. Now that's a party!

PIECE OF CAKE

NO-BAKE • MAKES 16 CAKE BITES

Sweet party pops look like perfect pieces of cake and are a piece of cake to make, too. Mini wedges of pound cake on forks are coated in melted vanilla frosting, with lines of red gel to create the layers.

1 frozen pound cake (16 ounces; Sara Lee Family Size), thawed
16 assorted colored plastic forks
Sugar
1 can (16 ounces) vanilla frosting
1 can (16 ounces) milk chocolate frosting
3 tubes (0.68 ounce each) red decorating gel (Cake Mate or Wilton)
2 tablespoons mini candy decors (Cake Mate)

1 Line two cookie sheets with waxed paper. Place the pound cake on a work surface with one long edge facing you. Using a serrated knife, cut the cake crosswise into quarters. Cut each quarter in half crosswise, then in half again on the diagonal to create four 1½-by-2½-inch triangles. Insert the tines of a plastic fork into the base of each piece of cake to secure, without breaking the cake. Transfer the pieces to the cookie sheets. Freeze for 15 minutes.

2 Fill several wide-mouthed glasses about three-quarters full with sugar to help support the cake pieces once they are frosted.

3 Spoon ¼ cup of the vanilla frosting into a ziplock bag. Spoon the chocolate frosting into 2 separate ziplock bags. Press out the excess air and seal the bags. Spoon the remaining vanilla frosting into a 2-cup glass measuring cup. Microwave, stopping to stir frequently, until it has the texture of lightly whipped cream, 20 to 30 seconds.

4 Remove the cake pieces from the freezer. Holding one of the pieces of cake by the fork over the measuring cup, spoon the melted frosting over the 2 long sides of the cake to cover, allowing the excess frosting to drip back into the cup. Insert the base of the fork into a sugar-filled glass. Repeat with the remaining cake pieces. If the melted frosting becomes too thick for spooning, microwave for several seconds and stir. Refrigerate the frosted cake pieces until set, about 20 minutes.

5 Use a toothpick to lightly score 2 lines in the frosting on each side of the cakes to mark the layers. Pipe a thin line of the red gel over each line.

6 Snip a medium (¼-inch) corner from the bags with the vanilla and chocolate frostings. Pipe a thin layer of chocolate frosting on the top and back of the cake pieces. Use the back of a small spoon to make swirls in the frosting. Pipe a dollop of vanilla frosting on top and add some candy decors.

7 Return the cake slices to the sugar-filled wide-mouthed glasses and serve.

EMOTIPOPS

NO-BAKE • MAKES 18 EXPRESSIONS

Little cakes on a fork sport emoticons with messages like ;-D (wink and a smile), d'-'b (I'm listening to my headphones), ( ) (cyber hug), or <3 (heart).

1 frozen pound cake (16 ounces; Sara Lee Family Size), thawed
18 plastic forks
¼ cup canned dark chocolate frosting
   Black, neon pink, red, yellow, and green food coloring (McCormick)
1 can (16 ounces) vanilla frosting
1 black licorice lace (see Sources)

1 Place the pound cake on a work surface. Trim ⅛ inch from each short end to straighten. Cut the cake into nine 1-inch-thick slices. Place a slice, cut side down, on the work surface and cut two 1¾-inch circles with a round cookie cutter or the rim of a small glass. Repeat with the remaining slices to make 18 cake circles (reserve the scraps for a layered dessert).

2 Line a cookie sheet with waxed paper. Carefully insert the tines of a plastic fork into one side of each cake circle to secure and place them on the cookie sheet. Freeze for 15 minutes.

3 Tint the dark chocolate frosting black with the black food coloring and spoon into a ziplock bag. Press out the excess air and seal. Divide the vanilla frosting among 4 microwavable bowls. Tint each bowl of frosting a different bright color of pink, orange (using red and yellow), yellow, and green with the food coloring. Cover the bowls with plastic wrap to prevent drying.

4 Working with one bowl of frosting at a time, microwave the frosting, stopping to stir frequently, until it has the texture of lightly whipped cream, about 10 seconds. Remove the cake pops from the freezer. Dip the cake into the melted frosting to cover, allowing the excess frosting to drip back into the bowl. Press the bottom of the cake circle against the rim of the bowl to remove any excess frosting and return to the cookie sheet. Repeat with the remaining cake pops and frosting (two colors will have 4 pops each and two colors will have 5 pops each). Refrigerate until the frosting is set, about 20 minutes.

5 Cut the licorice lace into ⅛-inch, ¼-inch, and ½-inch pieces. Snip a very small (1/16-inch) corner from the bag with the black frosting. For the eyes, use tweezers and a toothpick to press 2 of the smaller pieces of licorice, cut side down, into the frosting of each cake pop. Use more pieces of licorice, along with black frosting piped from the ziplock bag for round shapes, to create the emoticon symbols, using the photo as a guide. Transfer to a serving plate.

PUPPY LOVE POPS

NO-BAKE • MAKES 18 PUPS

Heart shapes cut from pound cake, placed on plastic forks, dipped in melted frosting, and decorated to look like adorable pups are perfect for a party because the forks make serving them so easy.

- 18 chocolate chews (Tootsie Rolls)
- 18 soft caramels (Kraft)
- 1 frozen pound cake (16 ounces; Sara Lee Family Size), thawed
- 18 light pink plastic forks
- ¼ cup graham cracker crumbs
- ¼ cup chocolate cookie crumbs (Oreos, Famous Chocolate Wafers)
- 1 can (16 ounces) vanilla frosting
- ¼ cup canned chocolate frosting
- 18 pink conversation hearts or small pink hearts
- 36 mini chocolate chips (Nestlé)
- 18 small red candies or mini candy-coated chocolates (Red Hots, M&M's Minis)

1 Line three cookie sheets with waxed paper. Microwave the chocolate chews and caramels for no more than 3 seconds to soften. Roll out each chew and caramel separately on a work surface into a 2-inch oval. Cut each oval into a teardrop shape for the ears. Transfer the ears to a cookie sheet.

2 Place the pound cake on a work surface. Trim ⅛ inch from each short end of the cake to straighten. Cut the cake crosswise into nine 1-inch-thick slices. Place a slice, cut side down, on the work surface and cut two 2-inch heart shapes with a cookie cutter (see Sources). Repeat with the remaining slices to make 18 cake hearts (reserve the scraps for a layered dessert).

3 Insert the tines of a plastic fork into the top of each cake heart to secure, without breaking the cake (see photo, page 142). Transfer to a cookie sheet and freeze for 15 minutes.

4 Place the graham cracker and chocolate cookie crumbs in separate shallow bowls. Spoon ¼ cup of the vanilla frosting into a ziplock bag. Press out the excess air and seal the bag. Mix the remaining vanilla frosting with the chocolate frosting in a microwavable bowl to make light brown frosting. Microwave, stopping to stir frequently, until the frosting has the texture of lightly whipped cream, 20 to 30 seconds.

5 Remove the cake hearts from the freezer. Holding the plastic fork, dip a cake heart into the melted frosting to cover, allowing the excess frosting to drip back into the bowl. Press the bottom of the cake heart against the rim of the bowl to remove any excess frosting. Sprinkle the frosted heart with spots of the graham cracker and chocolate cookie crumbs (see photo). Return to the cookie sheet. Repeat with the remaining cake hearts. If the melted frosting becomes too thick for dipping, microwave, stirring well, for about 5 seconds more.

6 For the tongue, press a conversation heart into the center of the rounded end of the cake heart. Snip a small (⅛-inch) corner from the bag with the vanilla frosting. For the eyes, pipe 2 dots of frosting on top of the cake and attach the mini chocolate chips, flat side up. For the nose, attach the red candy with a dot of frosting. Pipe a dot of vanilla frosting along each side of the cake and attach the small end of 2 of the flattened chews or caramels for the ears (after a few minutes, the ears will settle flat against the pops and the serving plate). Repeat with the remaining pups.

fork pops

Fork pops are perfect for parties because they're small and easy to serve. They are easy to make, too. Simply push the tines of a plastic fork into the side of the treat, freeze, dip, and decorate. You can use almost any treat as long as it's firm and hugs the tines.

- **A pound cake circle dipped into white frosting and decorated with a blue fruit chew, a Junior Mint, and licorice lace becomes an eyeball.**

- **Plain doughnut holes make great sports balls. For a basketball, dip into orange frosting and texture it with a paper towel. Add piped lines with black frosting for the stripes.**

- **Rice cereal treats can be shaped into cubes, dipped into frosting, and decorated with M&M's Minis to make dice.**

- **Brownies cut into little wedges make perfect slices of pizza. Add light brown frosting for the crust, red decorating gel tomato sauce, grated white chocolate cheese, and candy pepperoni and peppers.**

EGGS-TRA SPECIAL COOKIES

MAKES 1 DOZEN SANDWICH COOKIES

These egg-ceptional sandwich cookies, decorated on both sides with colorful egg-wash stripes, are as pretty as Fabergé eggs. The yolk is filled with rich yellow lemon curd.

2 **large eggs**
  Red, neon blue, neon green, green, and yellow food coloring (McCormick)
2 **recipes Quick Sugar Cookie Dough (page 226)**
  All-purpose flour
½ **recipe Royal Frosting (page 232)**
1 **jar (10 ounces) lemon curd**

1 Preheat the oven to 350°F. Line three cookie sheets with parchment paper.

2 Beat the eggs in a small bowl until well combined. Strain the beaten eggs through a fine sieve to remove any lumps. Divide the mixture among four small bowls. Tint each bowl a different color of red, neon blue, neon green, and green with the food coloring. Cover with plastic wrap and set aside.

3 Divide the cookie dough in half. Roll out one half on a lightly floured surface to a ⅛-inch thickness. Use a 4-inch egg-shaped cookie cutter (see Sources) to cut out 12 eggs, cutting as closely together as possible. Transfer the shapes to the cookie sheets about 1 inch apart. Using a round cookie cutter or a small knife, remove a 1½-inch circle from the center of the egg shapes. Refrigerate the egg shapes while you repeat with the remaining dough, but without cutting a circle from the shapes, rolling together the scraps as necessary.

egg-ceptional!

4 Removing only one cookie sheet from the refrigerator at a time, brush the tops of the egg shapes with tinted egg wash, using separate clean small paintbrushes for each color. Paint stripes, waves, or dots, leaving a ⅛-inch space between each color (see photo, page 144, for ideas). Trace a line between the colors with a toothpick to keep the colors from running together. For more intense colors, return the painted cookies to the refrigerator for 10 minutes and brush a second coat of the same color egg wash on top of the first coat.

5 Bake until the cookies are light golden and firm to the touch, 7 to 12 minutes. Transfer to a wire rack and cool completely. Repeat with the remaining cookies and egg wash.

6 Spoon the royal frosting into a ziplock bag. Press out the excess air and seal the bag. Snip a very small (1/16-inch) corner from the bag and pipe decorative lines and dots, outlining the colors, on top of the cookies. Allow the cookies to dry for at least 1 hour.

7 Just before serving, tint the lemon curd bright yellow with the food coloring. Spread some of the lemon curd over the undecorated side of each whole cookie. Sandwich with a cookie with a hole. Repeat with the remaining cookies and lemon curd. Arrange on a platter.

egg painting

Colorful egg washes can transform cookies and piecrust into vibrant decorations.

- Whisk an egg with a fork until it is well beaten, then strain through a fine sieve. Add food coloring and blend well.

- Use a small brush to paint the tinted egg wash onto the cookie or pie dough.

- Leave open space between each color and trace a line between the colors with a toothpick to keep the colors from running together.

- Refrigerate the dough after painting. When it is chilled, paint with a second coat for a more vibrant color.

- Bake the dough according to the directions in the recipe. Small cracks and slight browning add character to the colors.

BIRTHDAY TOWERS

MAKES 12 TOWERS; SERVES 36

The candles on these three-tiered towers of deliciousness only look as if they're on fire. Made from wheat sticks coated in pink chocolate, they have glowing orange and yellow frosting flames and are sure to ignite any party.

  3 cans (16 ounces each) vanilla frosting
    Yellow, red, neon green, and neon blue food coloring (McCormick)
 54 thin honey wheat sticks (Pringles) or thin pretzel sticks (Bachman)
  1 cup pink candy melting wafers (Wilton)
 ¼ cup white candy melting wafers (Wilton)
 12 jumbo cupcakes baked in foil liners (Reynolds)
 12 standard cupcakes baked in foil liners (Reynolds)
 12 mini cupcakes baked in foil liners (Reynolds)
 12 wooden skewers (4 inches long)

1 Place ¾ cup of the vanilla frosting into each of 3 separate bowls. Tint each bowl a separate bright color with the food coloring: bright orange with the yellow and red food coloring, neon green, and neon blue. Spoon each color into a separate ziplock bag. Press out the excess air and seal the bags. Tint ½ cup of the remaining vanilla frosting yellow with the food coloring. Snip a small (⅛-inch) corner from the bag with the orange frosting. Pipe a line of orange frosting down the inside of a ziplock bag and then fill it with the yellow frosting. Press out the excess air and seal the bag.

2 Line two cookie sheets with waxed paper. Cut the wheat sticks in half. Place the pink candy melting wafers in a glass bowl. Microwave for 10 seconds, stir, and repeat until the candies are melted and smooth, about 1 minute. Holding the wheat sticks by one end, dip into the melted pink candy, covering as much as possible and allowing the excess candy to drip back into the bowl. Transfer the coated wheat sticks to the cookie sheets. Refrigerate until set, about 5 minutes.

3 Place the white candy melting wafers in a ziplock bag (do not seal the bag). Microwave for 10 seconds to soften. Massage the candies in the bag, return to the microwave, and repeat until the candy is smooth, about 30 seconds. Press out the excess air and seal the bag.

4 Remove the wheat sticks from the refrigerator. Snip a very small (¹⁄₁₆-inch) corner from the bag with the white candy melts. Pipe thin diagonal lines, close together, over the coated sticks to look like stripes. Move the sticks before the white candy has set to prevent any stray lines attached to the waxed paper (see photo, next page). Let the candy set, about 5 minutes.

5 Trim the top of the cupcakes level using a serrated knife. Spread the remaining vanilla frosting on top of all of the cupcakes and smooth. Snip small (⅛-inch) corners from the bags with the neon green and neon blue frostings. Working with the orange frosting, pipe a beaded line (see photo, page 148) along the outer edges of 4 of each size cupcake. Repeat with the remaining cupcakes and the neon green and neon blue frostings.

6 Place a jumbo cupcake on a serving plate. Arrange a same-color standard-size cupcake in the center of the jumbo cupcake. Top with a same-color mini cupcake to create a tower. Press lightly to secure the cupcakes. Insert a wooden skewer, pointed end down, into the center of the mini cupcake and push down to the jumbo cupcake, twisting gently to press through the liners (push below the surface of the frosting of the mini cupcake). Repeat with the remaining cupcakes to make 12 towers.

7 Insert a wheat stick candle in the center of each mini cupcake to cover the hole made by the skewer. Insert 4 wheat stick candles around each of the bottom 2 cupcakes. Snip a small (⅛-inch) corner from the bag with the yellow and orange frosting. Pipe a swirl of frosting at the tip of each wheat stick candle to look like a flame.

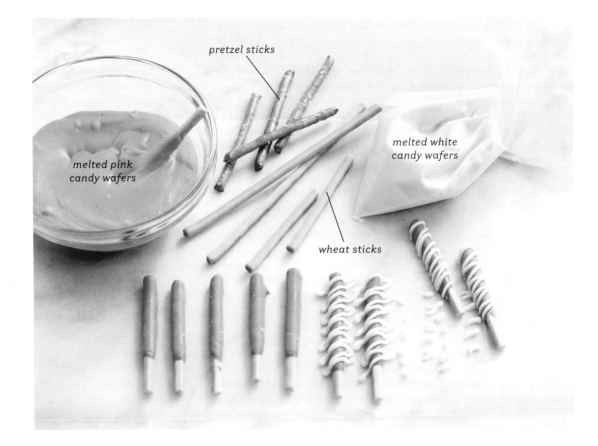

pretzel sticks

melted white
candy wafers

melted pink
candy wafers

wheat sticks

OCTOPUS GARDEN

MAKES 1 GARDEN; SERVES 24

There's a secret garden under the sea where store-bought meringue men-of-war and madeleine oysters with pearls sit in the shade of a measuring-cup octopus cake.

  8 anisette toasts (Stella D'oro)
  1 recipe Perfect Cake Mix (page 224), made with yellow cake, baked in a 2-cup oven-safe measuring cup and 16 cupcakes baked in gold foil liners (see Sources)
  2 cans (16 ounces each) vanilla frosting
  6 purple spice drops
  2 brown mini candy-coated chocolates (M&M's Minis)
  2 tablespoons purple decorating sugar (see Sources)
24 madeleine butter cakes (Entenmann's)
    Neon purple, blue, and neon pink food coloring (McCormick)
½ cup coarse white decorating sugar (Wilton)
16 each green and yellow licorice laces (see Sources)
24 red sour laces (Haribo Gummi Sour S'ghetti)
  8 pink meringue cookies
1½ cups graham cracker crumbs
¼ cup pearl candy-coated chocolate balls (Sixlets)
  3 green sour belts (Sour Power)
¼ cup white chocolate chips (Nestlé, Ghirardelli)
50 orange cereal O's (Apple Jacks)
  1 teaspoon blue decorating sugar (Cake Mate)

1 To give the octopus legs their crescent shape, use a serrated knife to remove a curved ½-inch-wide shape from the flat inside of the anisette toasts, following the outside curve as a guide. For the octopus body, trim the edges of the measuring-cup cake to round the top. Spread some of the vanilla frosting on top of the cake to smooth any lumps. For the eyes, remove ¼ inch from the round end of 2 of the purple spice drops and press the chocolate candies on the sticky round end and set aside. Press the trimmings and the remaining 4 purple spice drops together and roll out in the purple sugar to a ⅛-inch thickness, adding more sugar to prevent sticking. Cut the flattened spice drops into five ¾- to 1¼-inch spots and set aside.

2 For the oysters, line two cookie sheets with waxed paper. Place wire racks on top. Trim the bottom of the madeleines level with a serrated knife. Place the madeleines, trimmed side down, close together on a wire rack. Microwave 1 cup of the vanilla frosting in a 2-cup glass measuring cup, stopping to stir frequently, until it has the texture of lightly whipped cream, 25 to 30 seconds. Spoon the melted frosting over each madeleine to cover. Gather the excess frosting and return it to the measuring cup. Refrigerate the madeleines until set, about 30 minutes.

3 Add additional vanilla frosting to the melted frosting in the cup to measure about 1¼ cups. Tint the frosting purple with the neon purple and 1 drop of the blue food coloring. Microwave the purple frosting, stopping to stir frequently, until it has the texture of lightly whipped cream, 20 to 25 seconds. For the tentacles, dip each trimmed anisette toast into the frosting to cover completely, allowing the excess frosting to drip back into the cup. Place the toasts, inner curved side down, on a wire rack. Place the cake, large end up, on the wire rack. Pour the remaining purple frosting over the cake to cover completely. Refrigerate the cake and toasts until set, about 30 minutes.

4 Tint ½ cup of the remaining vanilla frosting pink with the food coloring. Spoon the pink frosting into a ziplock bag. Tint half of the remaining vanilla frosting light purple with the food coloring. Spoon 2 tablespoons of the light purple frosting into a ziplock bag. Press out the excess air and seal the bags.

5 To assemble the jellyfish, place the white decorating sugar in a shallow bowl. Cut the green and yellow licorice laces into 4- and 5-inch lengths. Spread the light purple frosting on top of 8 of the cupcakes and smooth. Roll the edges in the sugar. For the tentacles, arrange 3 or 4 pieces each of the yellow and green licorice laces on top of each cupcake, allowing them to hang over the edge. Add 3 pieces of the red sour laces for the stinging tentacles. For the jellyfish bodies, press a meringue onto each cupcake.

under the sea

6 To assemble the oysters, remove the madeleines from the wire rack and trim any excess frosting with a small knife. Place the graham cracker crumbs in a shallow bowl. Spread some of the remaining vanilla frosting on top of the remaining 8 cupcakes and smooth. Roll a wide edge on the sides of the cupcakes in the crumbs, leaving a small area of frosting to secure the oysters. For the bottom oyster shells, press one of the madeleines, frosted side down, on top of each cupcake. Snip a medium (¼-inch) corner from the bag with the pink frosting. Pipe a wavy line of frosting across the top of each madeleine for the oyster and add a pearl candy. Place another madeleine on top of each, frosted side up, and press into the pink frosting to secure. Repeat to make 4 extra oysters without cupcake bases. For the seaweed, cut the green sour belts into 2- to 2½-inch pieces. Cut small notches from a short end of each piece. Add some of the green sour belt pieces to the oyster cupcakes.

7 To assemble the octopus, transfer the purple frosted cake to a small serving plate. Place the white chocolate chips in a ziplock bag (do not seal the bag). Microwave for 10 seconds to soften. Massage the chips in the bag, return to the microwave, and repeat the process until the candy is smooth, about 30 seconds. Press out the excess air and seal the bag. Snip a small (⅛-inch) corner from the bag. Pipe some of the white chocolate on the ends of the frosted anisette toasts and arrange them as the tentacles around the base of the cake. Use a glass or can to help support the legs in upright positions while the chocolate is drying. Let stand for about 15 minutes to set.

8 Snip a small (⅛-inch) corner from the bag with the light purple frosting. For the suckers, pipe a line of light purple frosting along the inner curved side of each tentacle and attach 6 or 7 orange cereal O's. Attach the spice drop eyes and purple spots to the cake with some of the frosting. Sprinkle the plate with any extra white decorating sugar and the blue decorating sugar.

9 Arrange the cake and cupcakes on a tiered cake stand, allowing the licorice jellyfish tentacles to hang over the side. Sprinkle the lowest surface with some of the remaining graham cracker crumbs. Add the extra pearl candies and the 4 extra oysters.

SODA SHOP

MAKES 16 ICE CREAM SODAS

You can be a real jerk . . . soda jerk, that is. Cupcakes rise up tall with rounded crowns when baked in a popover pan. Dip them into melted frosting and add a dollop of frozen-frosting topping, straws, and sprinkles for old-time chocolate, vanilla, and strawberry ice cream sodas.

- 1 can (16 ounces) plus 1 cup vanilla frosting
  Red food coloring
- 2 tablespoons canned chocolate frosting
- 1 recipe Perfect Cake Mix (page 224), made with yellow cake and baked in popover pans in foil liners (Reynolds; 16 cupcakes)
- 1 tablespoon white sprinkles (Wilton)
- 2 tablespoons coarse white decorating sugar (Wilton)
- 16 white and red bendy straws, bottom 4 inches removed
- 1 teaspoon unsweetened cocoa powder
- 5–6 large pink decors (Wilton)
- 1 tablespoon chocolate sprinkles
- 16 red and white cupcake girdles (page 158)

1 Spoon ¾ cup of the vanilla frosting into a small bowl and freeze for at least 30 minutes.

2 Divide the remaining vanilla frosting among 3 small microwavable bowls. Tint one bowl pink with the red food coloring. Add the chocolate frosting to one bowl and stir well to combine. Leave the third bowl white. Cover each bowl with plastic wrap to prevent drying.

3 Working with one color of frosting, microwave the frosting, stopping to stir frequently, until it has the texture of lightly whipped cream, 10 to 15 seconds. Holding a cupcake by the liner, dip it into the melted frosting up to the liner, allowing the excess frosting to drip back into the bowl. Transfer to a cookie sheet. While the frosting is still wet, top the cupcake with some of the white sprinkles or decorating sugar. Repeat with 4 more cupcakes. Repeat the process with 5 cupcakes for each color frosting (for one color, dip 1 additional cupcake).

- Cut the girdle shape from your paper using the template. You can increase the height as needed for your design.

cupcake girdles

Girdles make your cupcake treats extra pretty. A tight one grips the sides of the cupcake and makes it taller, while a loose one can be left more open at the top to reveal the cupcake liner inside. You will need crafting scissors for the decorative edge, semirigid but flexible patterned or solid-color paper (see Sources), transparent tape, and the template on the opposite page.

- Add a decorative edge to the top of the shape or cut freehand designs like grass or picket fencing.

- Wrap the girdle around a cupcake to measure the size and style, then tape it together.

4 Remove the vanilla frosting from the freezer and use a small spoon or mini ice cream scoop to shape the frozen frosting into balls. Place a scoop of frosting on top of each cupcake, pressing down slightly to secure. Insert a bendy straw into the top of each cupcake.

5 For the chocolate malts, dust the top of each cupcake with some of the cocoa powder. For the strawberry sodas, add a pink decor to the white frosting on top. For the vanilla creams, add the chocolate sprinkles.

6 Just before serving, place each cupcake into a paper girdle and arrange on a serving platter (because of the sleeves, they will be a little top-heavy, so if transporting, wait until you arrive to assemble).

soda jerk

YEAR OF THE DRAGON

MAKES 1 DRAGON; 19 CUPCAKES

Slay your guests with an over-the-top dragon for Chinese New Year. Three colors of candy clay made from white chocolate chips, a handful of mini breakfast treats, and a wafer ice cream cone are all it takes to put your cupcaking skills on parade.

  1 **wafer cup ice cream cone (Joy)**
  ½ **cup yellow decorating sugar (Cake Mate)**
  ¼ **cup light corn syrup (Karo)**
     15 mini breakfast treat cookies (Stella D'oro 100 Calorie Pack)
  2 **recipes Candy Clay (page 230), made with white chocolate chips**
     Red paste food coloring (Wilton)
     Yellow and green food coloring
  2 **black licorice laces (see Sources)**
  1 **can (16 ounces) vanilla frosting**
 19 **vanilla cupcakes baked in yellow or gold paper liners (see Sources)**
  2 **white flat candy wafers (Necco)**
  2 **each brown and green candy-coated chocolates (M&M's)**
  1 **tube (4.25 ounces) chocolate decorating icing (Cake Mate)**

1 For the dragon's head, cut a 1½-by-¾-inch wedge from the small end of the ice cream cone using a small serrated knife (see photo).

head   *spine*

2 Line a cookie sheet with waxed paper. Place the yellow sugar in a shallow bowl. Microwave the corn syrup in a small bowl until boiling, 5 to 10 seconds. For the dragon's head, brush the top and sides of the trimmed cone with a thin coating of the corn syrup and immediately dip it into the yellow sugar to coat. For the dragon's spine, brush 13 of the mini breakfast treats with the corn syrup and dip into the yellow sugar to coat. Transfer the sugared pieces to the cookie sheet and set aside the remaining 2 breakfast treats.

3 Tint 1 recipe of the candy clay bright red with the red paste food coloring (you may want to wear disposable gloves to prevent dyeing your hands). Tint half of the remaining clay yellow and the other half green with the food coloring. Keep the clay covered with plastic wrap to prevent drying.

4 Line three cookie sheets with waxed paper. Roll out half of the red candy clay between 2 sheets of waxed paper to a ⅛-inch thickness. Repeat with the other half of the red candy clay, and then the green and yellow candy clay. Cut out the template shapes (see opposite page) using a paring knife or cookie cutters (see Sources), rerolling the scraps as necessary to make the number indicated for each shape. Transfer the shapes to the cookie sheets and cover with plastic wrap to prevent drying.

5 For the firecrackers, roll the remaining red candy clay into a ½-inch-diameter rope. Cut the rope into seven 2-inch pieces. Cut the black licorice laces into seven 1½-inch lengths. Insert a piece of licorice in one short end of each red candy log for the fuse.

6 Spoon ¼ cup of the vanilla frosting into a ziplock bag. Press out the excess air and seal the bag. Tint the remaining vanilla frosting yellow with the food coloring.

7 Spread the yellow frosting on top of the cupcakes and smooth. For the body, arrange 6 green candy clay triangles on 13 of the cupcakes, 3 on each side, allowing the tips to hang over the edges by about 1 inch. Top each with a red candy clay scallop and a yellow burst, pressing lightly into the frosting to secure. Snip a small (⅛-inch) corner from the bag with the vanilla frosting. Pipe 2 small dots of frosting on top of each yellow burst and add a sugar-coated breakfast treat for the spine. For the leg cupcakes, arrange 2 of the yellow candy clay triangles on one side of 2 of the cupcakes, allowing the tips to hang over the edges by about 1 inch. Add a red and a green zigzag, overlapping the yellow triangles. Repeat the decoration on the opposite side of 2 more cupcakes. For the tail cupcake, add a yellow triangle and 2 green zigzags at one edge on one of the body cupcakes. For the neck cupcake, arrange 2 yellow and 3 green triangles on the front edge of the cupcake, allowing the tips to hang over by 1 to 1½ inches. Cut the remaining red scallop in half and place at the front edge of the cupcake, overlapping the yellow and green triangles.

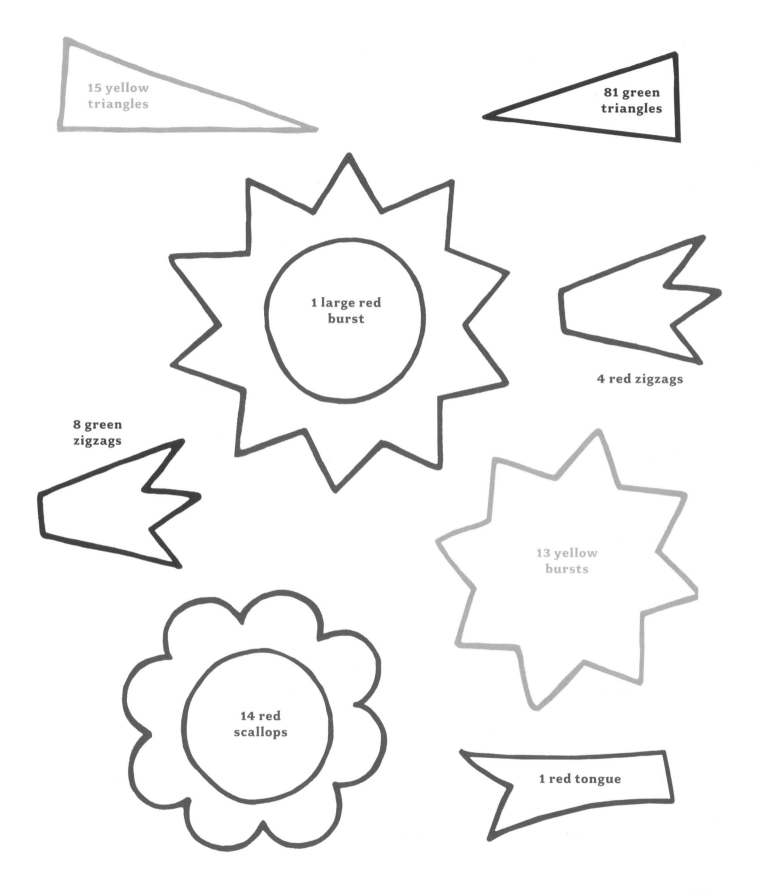

15 yellow triangles

81 green triangles

1 large red burst

4 red zigzags

8 green zigzags

13 yellow bursts

14 red scallops

1 red tongue

8 For the head, press the large red candy clay burst on top of the remaining cupcake. Arrange the remaining 4 yellow triangles on the top half of the cupcake as the ears and horns. Press the remaining 2 green zigzags below the yellow pieces on opposite sides of the cupcake. Pipe some of the vanilla frosting along the open end of the sugared cone and place it on the lower third of the cupcake. Attach the yellow candy clay ears and horns to the cut edges of the cone with some of the vanilla frosting. Attach the red candy clay tongue to the bottom edge of the cut portion of the cone. For the eyes, pipe 2 dots of frosting at the top edge of the cone and add the white candy wafers. Add the brown candies as the pupils, the green candies as the nostrils, and the 2 reserved breakfast treats as the eyebrows, each secured with a dot of frosting. Pipe the teeth with the vanilla frosting using the squeeze-release-pull technique (see page 75). Pipe the eyebrows with the chocolate decorating icing.

9 Arrange the neck and 13 body cupcakes on a large serving platter in an S shape, beginning with the neck cupcake and ending with the tail cupcake. Add 2 leg cupcakes, with the candy clay triangles pointing away from the body, on either side of the neck cupcake. Add the remaining 2 leg cupcakes on either side of the body between the third and fourth rear cupcakes. Pipe a dot of vanilla frosting on the back edge of the neck cupcake. Place the head cupcake on its side, on the back third of the neck cupcake, pressing it into the frosting and supported by the body cupcake behind it (if you are traveling with the cupcakes, wait until you are at the location to add the head cupcake).

10 Serve with the firecracker candies.

MONET'S WATER LILIES

MAKES 1 LILY POND; 12 MINI CUPCAKES

Make an impression with your own version of Monet's water lilies, created with white chocolate and the back of a plastic spoon. The candy petals are artfully placed on cupcake lily pads floating in a pool of cobalt-blue Jell-O.

> 2 packages (3 ounces each) blue gelatin dessert (Jell-O)
> 2 cups white candy melting wafers (Wilton)
>   Plastic spoons
> 1¼ cups canned vanilla frosting
>   Red and green food coloring
> 12 mini vanilla cupcakes
> 2 teaspoons yellow sprinkles

1 Follow the package directions for the blue gelatin dessert. Pour the prepared gelatin into a large shallow serving dish that can hold 1 quart. Refrigerate until the gelatin is set, at least 3 hours.

2 For the petals, line three cookie sheets with waxed paper. Place the white candy melts in a glass bowl. Microwave for 10 seconds, stir, and repeat until the candies are melted and smooth, about 1 minute. Dip the back of a plastic spoon (this needs to be plastic) into the melted candy to coat, making sure that the candy does not go over the edge of the spoon. Allow the excess candy to drip back into the bowl. Transfer the coated spoon, candy side up, to a cookie sheet. Repeat with more spoons (see photo). Refrigerate until set, about 5 minutes.

3 Remove the petals from the refrigerator and let stand for 1 minute. Carefully bend the backs of the spoons to release the candy. Transfer the candies to a cookie sheet. Any broken pieces can be melted again with the remaining candy. If the candy becomes too thick, return to the microwave and heat for 10 seconds, stirring frequently, until smooth. Repeat the dipping, chilling, and releasing steps to make about 80 petals. (The petals can be made up to 1 week in advance and stored in an airtight container.)

4 Tint ¼ cup of the vanilla frosting pale pink with the red food coloring. Spoon the pink frosting into a ziplock bag. Press out the excess air and seal the bag. Tint the remaining frosting bright green with the food coloring.

5 Line a cookie sheet with waxed paper. Spoon any extra melted candy into a ziplock bag (do not seal the bag). Microwave for 5 seconds, massage the candy in the bag, return to the microwave, and repeat the process until the candy is smooth, about 20 seconds. Press out the excess air and seal the bag.

6 For the flower, snip a small (⅛-inch) corner from the bag with the melted candy. Pipe a dot of melted candy the size of a dime onto the waxed paper–lined cookie sheet. Arrange 3 to 5 of the candy petals, overlapping slightly, with the larger end of each petal in the melted candy, to make the flower shape (see photo). Repeat to make about 15 flowers. Refrigerate until set, about 5 minutes.

7 Snip a small (⅛-inch) corner from the bag with the pink frosting and pipe the centers of the flowers (see photo) using the squeeze-release-pull technique (see page 75). Sprinkle with the yellow sprinkles. Use a 1½-inch round cookie cutter or a paring knife to cut out eight 1½-inch circles from the chilled gelatin. Spread the green frosting on top of the mini cupcakes. Remove the paper liners from 8 of the cupcakes and place in the openings in the gelatin. Arrange the flowers on top of the mini cupcakes, pressing into the frosting to secure, and add some flowers to the gelatin surface.

8 Serve the extra mini cupcakes and flowers with the gelatin.

make an impression

DAD'S STUFFED SHIRT

MAKES ONE 10½-BY-15½-INCH JELLY-ROLL CAKE AND 5 CUPCAKES; ABOUT 16 SERVINGS

If Dad's the pinstripe type, maybe it's time for a change. Five holes cut out of a sheet cake hold the cupcakes that stuff the shirt and support the graham-cracker tie. And don't forget he loves #2 pencils, made out of taffy.

- 1 can (16 ounces) plus 1 cup vanilla frosting
- 3 tablespoons canned dark chocolate frosting
  Black and blue food coloring (McCormick)
- 15 red fruit chews (Jolly Rancher)
- 10 yellow fruit chews, 1 pink, and 1 green (Laffy Taffy)
- 5 graham crackers
- 1 cup blue decorating sugar (Cake Mate)
- 1 recipe Perfect Cake Mix (page 224), made with yellow cake, baked
  in a 10½-by-15½-inch jelly-roll pan and 5 cupcakes baked in white paper liners
- 4 white flat candies (Smarties)

1 Spoon ¼ cup of the vanilla frosting into a ziplock bag. Tint the chocolate frosting black with the black food coloring. Spoon the black frosting into a ziplock bag. Press out the excess air and seal the bags. Tint the remaining vanilla frosting light blue with the blue food coloring. Cover the frosting with plastic wrap to prevent drying.

2 Line two cookie sheets with waxed paper. Microwave the 15 red and 9 of the yellow fruit chews for no more than 3 seconds to soften. Press three like-colored fruit chews together and roll out on a work surface to a 5-by-1-inch strip. Repeat with the remaining red and yellow chews. Trim the edges of the strips with a sharp knife to straighten and make them ¾ inch wide. Cut the yellow strips in half lengthwise. For the tie stripes, center a yellow strip on top of a red strip and press lightly to adhere. Cut 1 stripe in half crosswise; you will have 4 long stripes and 2 short stripes. Transfer to a cookie sheet. Microwave the remaining 3 fruit chews (yellow, pink, and green) for no more than 3 seconds to soften. Make a pencil about 1½ inches long by cutting and molding the chews with your hands (see photo). Transfer to a cookie sheet.

3 Use a small serrated knife to cut the graham crackers following the templates on page 170. Place the blue sugar in a shallow bowl. Working on one cracker piece at a time, spread some of the light blue frosting on the top and sides and smooth. Press the cracker into the blue sugar to cover the top and sides completely. Transfer the sugared cracker to the pan. Repeat with the remaining crackers.

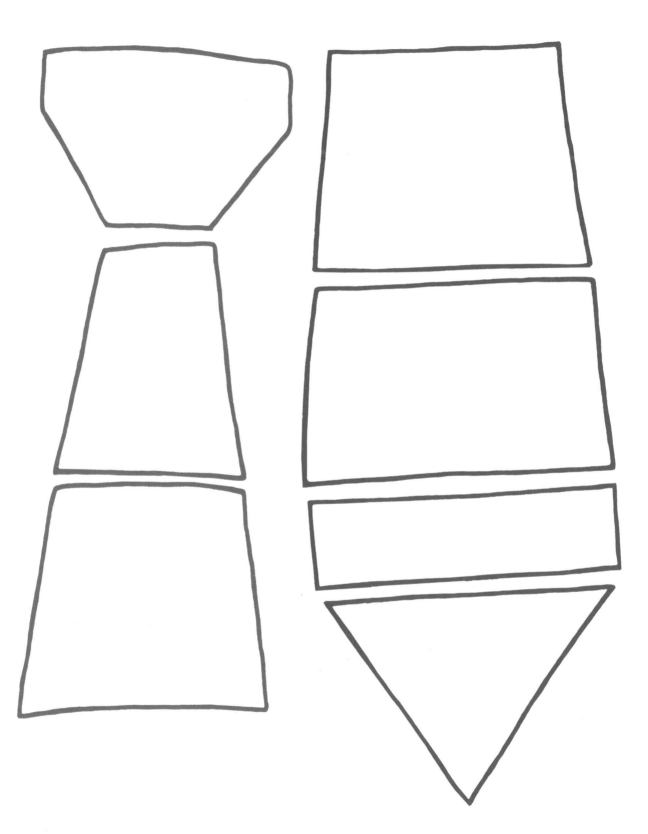

4 Trim the top of the cake and cupcakes level with a serrated knife. Transfer the cake, trimmed side down (the bottom side is flatter), to a serving platter. Use a 2½-inch round cookie cutter, the rim of a glass, or a small knife to remove five 2½-inch circles lengthwise down the center of the cake, about ½ inch apart (see photo). Spread the top and sides of the cake with some of the blue frosting and make as smooth as possible (leave the cutouts unfrosted).

5 Snip a small (⅛-inch) corner from the bags with the vanilla and black frostings. For the collar, use a toothpick to mark 3½-inch triangles on either side of the top hole cut out of the cake. Mark the lines for the 3-inch pocket with the toothpick. Pipe the black frosting to outline the collar, pocket, 4 buttonholes, and shirtfront. Use the vanilla frosting to pipe the white pinstripes about ¾ inch apart, using the photo as a guide. For the buttons, attach the flat white candies and pipe 4 dots of vanilla frosting as stitching.

6 Spread the remaining blue frosting on top of the cupcakes and smooth. Place the cupcakes in the openings on top of the cake. Wrap the fruit chew tie stripes around the sugared graham crackers (see photo, page 169), using the longer stripes for the wide part of the tie and the shorter stripes for the knot. Secure with dots of vanilla frosting and trimming any excess fruit chew. Arrange the crackers on top of the cupcakes in the tie shape, making sure that they are level. Add the fruit chew pencil to the pocket and press into the frosting to secure.

holidazed

There's gnome place like gnome for the holidays, where heartwarming treats like bloody bandages and zombies for Halloween, Puritans and leaf raking for Thanksgiving, and overstuffed stockings hanging by the fire make the season bright.

TURKEY VULTURES

MAKES 6 SCAVENGER CUPCAKES AND 6 ROCKS; 12 SERVINGS

Let's pick up dinner at that new place out on the highway! These squirm-worthy Halloween treats are crafted from a cupcake and a mini doughnut covered in frosting, with a doughnut hole dipped in melted pink frosting for the creepy bald head.

VULTURES

- 1 **can (16 ounces) dark chocolate frosting**
- 6 **chocolate cupcakes baked in black paper liners (see Sources)**
- 6 **chocolate-frosted mini doughnuts**
- 6 **plain doughnut holes (Munchkins)**
- 12 **thin chocolate cookies (Famous Chocolate Wafers)**
- 12 **yellow banana-shaped hard candies (Runts)**
  Black and neon pink food coloring (McCormick)
- 1 **cup canned vanilla frosting**
- 12 **mini chocolate chips (Nestlé)**
- 1 **tablespoon chocolate sprinkles**

1 Spread some of the dark chocolate frosting on top of one of the cupcakes and place a mini doughnut on top, close to one edge. Attach a doughnut hole on top of the mini doughnut with more of the frosting. Repeat with the remaining cupcakes. Freeze until firm, about 20 minutes.

Parts   Build   Freeze   Dip

2 For the vulture tails, using a serrated knife and angling it slightly inward from top to bottom, cut ½ inch from opposite sides of 6 of the cookies. For the wings, cut the remaining 6 cookies in half and round one corner. For the feet, cut 6 of the banana-shaped candies in half.

3 Tint the remaining chocolate frosting black with the food coloring. Spoon ½ cup of the vanilla frosting into a ziplock bag. Press out the excess air and seal the bag. Tint the remaining vanilla frosting pink with the pink food coloring. Microwave the pink frosting in a small microwavable bowl, stirring frequently, until it has the texture of lightly whipped cream, 10 to 20 seconds. Holding a chilled cupcake by the liner, dip just the doughnut hole into the pink frosting to cover completely, allowing the excess frosting to drip back into the bowl. Turn right side up and set aside. Repeat with the remaining cupcakes.

4 Spread some of the black frosting over each cupcake and mini doughnut, up to the pink doughnut hole. Starting at an outside edge of the cupcake, make spikes by using a fork to gently pull the frosting away from the cupcake. Continue with overlapping rows, ending at the base of the pink doughnut hole. Repeat with the remaining cupcakes.

5 Attach a cookie wing on each side of the cupcake, rounded corner up and cut edges facing forward. Press the narrow end of the tail cookie into the frosting on the back of the cupcake, allowing it to hang over about 1 inch. Snip a small (⅛-inch) corner from the bag with the vanilla frosting. For the chest feathers, pipe overlapping rows of vanilla frosting on the front of the cupcake under the pink doughnut hole, using the squeeze-release-pull technique (see page 75). For the eyes, pipe 2 dots of vanilla frosting on the pink doughnut hole. Attach a mini chocolate chip, flat side out, to the frosting for each pupil. Use tweezers to add a chocolate sprinkle above each mini chip for the eyebrows. Press a pointed end of a whole banana candy into the doughnut hole head for the beak. For the feet, attach 2 cut banana candy pieces to the paper liner at the base of the cupcake with some chocolate frosting, cut sides in.

ROCKS

6 anisette toasts (Stella D'oro)

8 pretzel twists (Bachman)

¾ cup canned vanilla frosting

 Black food coloring (McCormick)

1½ cups canned chocolate frosting

6 chocolate cupcakes baked in black paper liners (see Sources)

¾ cup chocolate cookie crumbs (Oreos, Famous Chocolate Wafers)

1 Line a cookie sheet with waxed paper and place a wire rack on top. Break the anisette toasts into random 2-inch pieces. Break the pretzels into random large pieces. Tint the vanilla frosting gray with a drop of black food coloring.

2 Microwave ½ cup of the chocolate frosting in a small microwavable bowl, stirring frequently, until it has the texture of lightly whipped cream, 5 to 10 seconds. Dip the broken pretzels into the frosting to cover completely. Remove from the frosting with a fork, allowing the excess frosting to drip back into the bowl. Transfer to the wire rack. Repeat with the remaining pieces of pretzel. Refrigerate until set, about 20 minutes.

3 Spread the remaining chocolate frosting on top of the cupcakes and smooth. Microwave the gray frosting in a small microwavable bowl, stirring frequently, until it has the texture of lightly whipped cream, 10 to 15 seconds. Dip the broken cookies into the gray frosting to cover completely. Remove from the frosting with a fork, allowing the excess to drip back into the bowl. Transfer several pieces to the tops of the cupcakes, pressing into the frosting to secure (place any extra around the cupcakes). Let stand 15 minutes to set.

4 Sprinkle the tops of the cupcakes, around the cookie rocks, with the chocolate cookie crumbs to look like dirt. Insert several pieces of pretzel on top of the cupcakes to look like branches. Serve with the vultures.

DAY OF THE DEAD

NO-BAKE • MAKES 8 TREATS

Got brains? Inspired by the fanciful designs of Día de los Muertos *(Day of the Dead), crispy rice cereal treat skulls are served in ice cream cones. Make plenty because these are perfect Halloween snacks, too.*

8 wafer cup ice cream cones (Joy)
   Nonstick cooking spray
2 recipes Rice Cereal Treats (page 229)
½ cup white chocolate chips (Nestlé, Ghirardelli)
1 cup canned dark chocolate frosting
1 small bag (2 ounces) candy-coated chocolates (M&M's)
1 bag (12 ounces) mini candy-coated chocolates (M&M's Minis)
8 assorted color jumbo cupcake liners (see Sources)

1 Using a serrated knife, cut a 1-inch piece from the base of each cone (you will be using the top part for the skulls).

2 Line a cookie sheet with waxed paper. Spray your clean hands liberally with the nonstick cooking spray. Shape about ¾ cup of the rice cereal treat into a lightbulb shape with your hands. Make indentations for the eye sockets using your thumbs or the back of a greased spoon. Make sure to press firmly to create the shape and check that the tapered base of the lightbulb shape will fit into the top of the cone. Transfer to the cookie sheet. Repeat with the remaining rice cereal treat to make 8 skulls.

3 Place the white chocolate chips in a ziplock bag (do not seal the bag). Microwave for 10 seconds to soften, massage the chips in the bag, return to the microwave, and repeat the process until smooth, about 30 seconds. Press out the excess air and seal the bag.

4 Snip a small (⅛-inch) corner from the bag. Pipe some of the melted white chocolate along the inside rim of a trimmed cone. Insert a cereal skull, tapered end into the cone, reshaping if necessary, and secure. Return to the cookie sheet, standing upright. Repeat with the remaining rice cereal treats and cones. Refrigerate for about 10 minutes, or until set.

5 Arrange the decorated rice cereal skulls in the colored paper liners.

6 Spoon the dark chocolate frosting into a ziplock bag. Press out the excess air and seal the bag. Snip a small (⅛-inch) corner from the bag. Pipe a dot of frosting in the center of each eye socket and pipe small lines of frosting radiating out from the center. Pipe a dot at the end of each radiating line and in patterns of your choice on the rest of the rice cereal treat (see photo). Attach 2 same-color large candies at the center of the sockets for the eyes and mini candies in contrasting colors on the remaining dots. For the nose, pipe a small upward-pointing triangle at the top edge of each cone and attach 3 same-color mini candies. For the mouth, pipe an upward-curving oval on the lower part of each cone, fill in the shape with additional lines of frosting, and attach same-color mini candies to fill in the shape.

día de los muertos

BANDAGES AND SCARS

MAKES 20 BANDAGE COOKIES AND 24 SCAR CUPCAKES

Bloody, flesh-colored cookies will haunt you even after you know that the ooze comes from strawberry jam and the bruises on the scar cupcakes are the result of injecting jam into the center before baking. Not for the squeamish.

BANDAGES
Red food coloring
1 **recipe Quick Sugar Cookie Dough (page 226)**
All-purpose flour
½ **cup low-sugar strawberry preserves (Smucker's)**

1 Preheat the oven to 350°F. Line two cookie sheets with parchment paper.

2 Knead 4 drops of the red food coloring into the sugar cookie dough until well blended. Divide the dough in half. Roll out half of the dough on a lightly floured surface to a ⅛-inch thickness. Cut the dough into strips 1½ inches wide. Cut each strip into 5-inch lengths. Transfer the pieces to a cookie sheet about 1 inch apart. Reroll the scraps with the other half of the dough and repeat to make about 20 pieces. Use a small knife to round the corners to make the bandage shape. Poke rows of holes in the dough strips with the tines of a fork, leaving the center 1½ inches plain (see photo). Reroll the scraps and cut the remaining dough into twenty 1½-inch squares.

3 Spoon ½ teaspoon of the strawberry preserves in the center of a strip of dough. Moisten the edges of a small square of dough and cover the preserves, moistened edges down, pressing lightly to seal. Repeat with the remaining dough and preserves to make about 20 bandages.

4 Bake in batches until the cookies are lightly golden, 10 to 12 minutes. Transfer to a wire rack and cool completely.

SCARS

- 1 recipe Perfect Cake Mix (page 224), made with vanilla cake
  Red food coloring
- 24 white paper liners
- 1 cup low-sugar strawberry preserves (Smucker's)
- 2 tubes (0.68 ounce each) red decorating gel (Cake Mate)
- 1 tube (4.25 ounces) chocolate decorating icing (Cake Mate)

1 Prepare the Perfect Cake Mix through step 2. Tint the batter pink with several drops of red food coloring. Continue with the recipe, but fill the 24 paper liners only one-third full with the batter. Spoon 2 teaspoons strawberry preserves on top of the cake batter in each liner, then fill with the remaining cake batter. Bake and cool as directed.

2 Using a small paring knife, cut a jagged line into the top of one of the cupcakes. Pipe some of the red gel into the cut to look like blood. Pipe lines of the chocolate icing crosswise over the gel to look like stitches. Repeat with the remaining cupcakes. Arrange the cupcakes and bandage cookies on a serving platter.

NIGHT OF THE LIVING CUPCAKE

MAKES 16 MONSTERS: 8 FRANKENSTEINS AND 8 ZOMBIES

Frankenstein meets the zombies, and everyone gets eaten for dessert! The misshapen torsos bulging over the liners of the monsters come from baking cupcakes in a popover pan. Did someone lose an arm?

- 8 **chocolate cookie sticks (Oreo Fun Stix)**
- 9 **vanilla cookie sticks (Golden Oreo Fun Stix, Pirouettes)**
  Toothpicks
- 24 **marshmallows**
- 62 **violet licorice pastels (Jelly Belly)**
- 56 **light green licorice pastels (Jelly Belly)**
- 16 **each green, brown, and yellow mini candy-coated chocolates (M&M's Minis)**
- 2 **cans (16 ounces each) vanilla frosting**
  Neon pink, green, yellow, and neon purple food coloring (McCormick)
- 1 **can (16 ounces) dark chocolate frosting**
- 16 **cupcakes, baked in popover pans (see page 225), 8 with black paper liners, 8 with dark blue paper liners (Reynolds)**
- ½ **cup chocolate cookie crumbs (Oreos; optional)**

1 Using a serrated knife, cut the chocolate and vanilla cookie sticks into 2-inch lengths, 16 chocolate and 18 vanilla. Insert a toothpick into the center of 16 marshmallows, 8 into the rounded side and 8 into the flat side (see photo). Cut the remaining 8 marshmallows in half lengthwise with scissors and insert a toothpick into the flat end. Cut 18 of the violet and 16 of the green licorice pastels in half crosswise. Cut off the top third of the green mini chocolate candies.

2 Line a cookie sheet with waxed paper. Spoon ½ cup of the vanilla frosting into a ziplock bag. Tint 2 tablespoons of the remaining vanilla frosting pink with the neon pink food coloring and spoon into a ziplock bag. Spoon 1 cup vanilla frosting into a microwavable glass bowl. Tint half of the remaining vanilla frosting pale green with the green and yellow food coloring, and tint the remaining vanilla frosting light purple with the neon purple food coloring. Spoon 2 tablespoons of the green frosting into a ziplock bag. Press out the excess air and seal the bags. Cover the bowls of frosting with plastic wrap to prevent drying. Working with the remaining green and the purple frosting, one color frosting at a time, microwave in a small microwavable bowl, stopping to stir frequently, until it has the texture of lightly whipped cream, 10 to 15 seconds. For the Frankenstein heads, dip a whole marshmallow with the toothpick on the flat side, holding it by the toothpick, into the light green melted frosting to cover completely, allowing the excess to drip back into the bowl (see photo, page 183). Press the bottom of the marshmallow against the rim of the bowl to remove any excess frosting and transfer to the cookie sheet. Repeat with the remaining 7 same marshmallows. For the zombie heads, repeat the dipping process with the whole marshmallows with the toothpick on the rounded side and the purple melted frosting.

3 Spoon ¾ cup of the dark chocolate frosting into a ziplock bag. Press out the excess air and seal the bag. Microwave the remaining dark chocolate frosting in a small microwavable bowl, stopping to stir frequently, until it has the texture of lightly whipped cream, 15 to 20 seconds. For the Frankenstein feet, hold a cut marshmallow by the toothpick and dip it into the chocolate melted frosting to cover completely (see photo, page 183), allowing the excess frosting to drip back into the bowl. Press the cut side of the marshmallow against the rim of the bowl to remove any excess frosting and transfer to the cookie sheet, cut side down. Repeat with the remaining cut marshmallows. For the torso, hold a black cupcake by the liner and dip it into the frosting up to the liner, allowing the excess frosting to drip back into the bowl. Transfer to a cookie sheet. Refrigerate the coated marshmallows and cupcakes until set, about 20 minutes.

4 For the zombie torsos and arms, microwave the vanilla frosting in the glass bowl, stopping to stir frequently, until it has the texture of lightly whipped cream, 15 to 20 seconds. Hold a dark blue cupcake by the liner and dip it into the vanilla frosting up to the liner, allowing the excess frosting to drip back into the bowl. Transfer to a cookie sheet. Repeat with the remaining dark blue cupcakes and the vanilla cookie sticks. Transfer to a cookie sheet. Refrigerate until set, about 20 minutes.

5　For the Frankensteins, snip a small (⅛-inch) corner from the bags with the chocolate, vanilla, and green frostings. For the arms, pipe a dot of chocolate frosting on each end of the chocolate cookie sticks. Place a brown candy at one end and 2½ green licorice pastels at the other for the fingers. Repeat with the remaining chocolate cookies. Pipe the lapels with the chocolate frosting on one side of each black cupcake (see photo, page 185). Carefully remove the toothpick from one of the green marshmallow heads and attach the marshmallow, flat side down, on top of the cupcake with a dot of chocolate frosting. For the eyes, pipe dots of the vanilla frosting on the marshmallow and attach the cut green chocolates, cut side up. Pipe a dot of the green frosting on each side of the marshmallow and attach a green licorice pastel half for the bolts. Pipe dots of the green frosting above the eyes and attach a whole green licorice pastel.

6　Using a plastic bench scraper or spatula, squeegee the chocolate frosting to the uncut corner of the ziplock bag. Tape shut the first corner. Snip a very small (¹⁄₁₆-inch) corner from the new corner. Pipe the hair, scar, mouth, and pupils with the frosting. Pipe a dot of chocolate frosting on each side of the cupcake and attach the cookie arms, pressing to secure. Repeat with the remaining black cupcakes. Arrange on a serving platter and place 2 chocolate-covered marshmallow halves in front of each cupcake for the feet (remove and discard the toothpicks).

7　For the zombies, snip a small (⅛-inch) corner from the bag with the pink frosting. For the arms and hands, pipe a dot of vanilla frosting on one end of each of the dipped vanilla cookie sticks. Place 2 whole and 2 half violet licorice pastels into the frosting for the fingers. Repeat with the remaining 17 cookies. Pipe the lapels and tie on one side of the dark blue cupcake with the vanilla and chocolate frostings (see photo). Attach the arms with vanilla frosting (you will have 2 extra arms). For the head, carefully remove the toothpick from a purple marshmallow and attach the marshmallow, rounded side down and flat side forward, on top of the cupcake with a dot of vanilla frosting. For the eyes, pipe dots of the vanilla frosting on the flat side of the marshmallow and attach the yellow candies. For the eyebrows, attach a violet licorice pastel above the eyes with dots of vanilla frosting. Pipe a wavy line of pink frosting for the mouth. Pipe dots of white frosting for the teeth, using the squeeze-release-pull technique (see page 75). Pipe spiky patches of hair on top of the marshmallow with the chocolate frosting and pupils on the yellow candies. Fill in areas on the top of the head with some of the pink frosting to look like brains.

8　Repeat with the remaining 7 cupcakes. Sprinkle a serving platter with the cookie crumbs as dirt, if desired. Add the 2 extra arms to the serving platter.

SPIDER BITES

MAKES 20 SPIDERS

Arachnophobes needn't worry about touching these brownie pops with chocolate legs on a white chocolate web: just pick up the fork and stick one in your mouth.

  1 **recipe Perfect Brownie Mix (page 228), baked in a 9-by-13-inch pan**
 20 **violet plastic forks (see Sources)**
  2 **cups chopped chocolate cookies (Oreos, chocolate graham crackers, Famous Chocolate Wafers)**
  1 **can (16 ounces) plus 1 cup chocolate frosting**
  1 **bag (14 ounces) plus 1 cup white candy melting wafers (Wilton)**
    Large red and purple sprinkles (Wilton)
  ½ **cup canned vanilla frosting**

1 Line a cookie sheet with waxed paper. Remove the whole brownie from the pan and remove the foil. Using a small knife or a 1½-inch round cookie cutter, cut out as many circles as possible from the brownie, reserving the scraps (you should have 20 circles). Transfer the circles to the cookie sheet. Gently insert a plastic fork into the top of each brownie circle, on the back edge (see photo), and refrigerate until ready to assemble.

2 Pulse the brownie scraps in a food processor until finely chopped. Transfer to a medium bowl. Add the chopped cookies to the food processor and pulse until ground. Transfer the cookie crumbs to a shallow bowl.

3 Spoon ½ cup of the chocolate frosting into a ziplock bag. Press out the excess air and seal the bag. Spoon ¾ cup of the remaining chocolate frosting into the bowl with the brownie crumbs and stir until the mixture holds together. For the spider heads, shape the mixture into twenty 1-inch balls. Press the balls into the cookie crumbs to coat, then flatten slightly.

4 Spoon the remaining chocolate frosting into a 2-cup glass measuring cup. Microwave, stopping to stir frequently, until it has the texture of lightly whipped cream, 20 to 30 seconds. Holding a chilled brownie circle by the fork, dip the brownie into the melted frosting to cover completely, allowing the excess frosting to drip back into the bowl. Transfer the brownie to the cookie crumbs and coat completely. Return to the cookie sheet. Repeat with the remaining brownies. If the melted frosting becomes too thick for dipping, microwave for several seconds, then stir.

5 For the legs, line two cookie sheets with waxed paper. Place the leg template (see page 190) under the waxed paper. Place 1 cup of the white candy melts into a ziplock bag (do not seal the bag). Microwave for 10 seconds to soften, massage the wafers in the bag, return to the

microwave, and repeat the process until the candy is smooth, about 60 seconds. Press out the excess air and seal the bag.

6 Snip a small (⅛-inch) corner from the bag with the melted candy. Pipe an outline of the leg template. Repeat to make several legs. Before the candy hardens, sprinkle with some of the chocolate cookie crumbs to cover. Repeat to make 8 legs for each spider, 4 in each direction (for a total of 160 legs). Refrigerate until the candy is set, about 5 minutes. Remove any excess cookie crumbs and reserve for another use.

7 Use a toothpick to make 4 small holes for the legs on opposite sides of each brownie, near the top. Working on one spider at a time, pipe a small dot of melted candy in each hole. Gently peel the candy legs from the waxed paper and press into the holes, adding more of the cookie crumbs to cover. Snip a small (⅛-inch) corner from the bag with the chocolate frosting. Pipe a vertical line of chocolate frosting on the front side of the brownie and add 3 red sprinkles for the spider's venom. For the head, attach a flattened brownie ball on top of the brownie with a dot of chocolate frosting. Repeat with the remaining brownies.

8 Spoon the vanilla frosting into a ziplock bag. Snip a small (⅛-inch) corner from the bag. Pipe 4 dots for the eyes on top of the head and 2 fangs, using the squeeze-release-pull technique (see page 75). Add the purple sprinkles as the pupils.

9 For the webs, line four cookie sheets with waxed paper. Divide the remaining white candy melts between two ziplock bags (do not seal the bags). Working with one bag at a time, microwave for 10 seconds to soften. Massage the wafers in the bag, return to the microwave, and repeat the process until the candy is smooth, about 60 seconds. Press out the excess air and seal the bag.

10 Snip a small (⅛-inch) corner from the bag. Working on one web at a time, pipe three intersecting lines 5 inches long (see photo, page 51). Connect the ends of each line with a piped swag. Pipe an additional swag halfway to the center point. While the candy is still wet, transfer a spider to the web, making sure the legs are attached to the web. Repeat to make one web for each spider, using both bags of candy melts. Refrigerate until set, about 10 minutes.

11 With a metal spatula, carefully peel the spiders and webs from the waxed paper before serving.

LEAF PIE-L

MAKES ONE 9-INCH AUTUMN PIE; ABOUT 12 SERVINGS

This pie-L of leaves will make you want to dive in and start eating. Leaf shapes cut from pastry dough get a colorful egg wash before baking. Rake them up with pie dough tines and a sugared bread-stick handle.

3 rolls (1½ boxes; 14.1 ounces each) refrigerated pie dough (Pillsbury)
  All-purpose flour
1 can (15 ounces) pumpkin puree
½ cup plus 3 teaspoons granulated sugar
½ cup packed light brown sugar
2 teaspoons pumpkin pie spice (McCormick)
¼ teaspoon salt
1 can (12 ounces) evaporated milk
2 large eggs
2 large egg whites
2 teaspoons red decorating sugar (Cake Mate)
1 plain bread stick, 6 inches long
  Pinch of ground cinnamon
  Red, green, and yellow food coloring
1 piece (7 inches) strawberry fruit leather (Fruit by the Foot)

1 Adjust the oven rack to the lower third of the oven. Preheat the oven to 425°F. For the pie, roll out 1 roll of the refrigerated pie dough on a lightly floured work surface to an 11-inch circle. Transfer the pie dough to a 9-inch pie plate. Fold the excess pie dough under at the rim to make a clean edge. Crimp the edge. Place the pie shell in the refrigerator until you are ready to fill and bake.

2 Combine the pumpkin puree, ½ cup of the granulated sugar, the brown sugar, pumpkin pie spice, salt, evaporated milk, and whole eggs. Beat with a whisk until well combined and smooth.

3 Remove the pie shell from the refrigerator and fill with the pumpkin mixture. Bake for 15 minutes. Reduce the oven temperature to 350°F. Continue baking until the center is just set, 40 to 50 minutes longer. Transfer the pie to a wire rack to cool.

4 For the rake, increase the oven temperature to 400°F. Line three cookie sheets with parchment paper. Beat the egg whites until well blended. Roll out 1 roll of the refrigerated pie dough on a lightly floured work surface to an 11-inch circle. Cut the dough into ten ½-by-6-inch strips. On a cookie sheet, arrange 9 of the strips into the shape of the rake head, overlap-

ping the top of the strips of dough and leaving ¼ inch between the strips at the bottom. Lean the bottom ½ inch of the strips on one edge of the cookie sheet to create the curved tines (see photo). Sprinkle the dough with 1 teaspoon of the remaining granulated sugar. Brush the remaining strip of dough with some of the beaten egg white and sprinkle with the red decorating sugar. Place the red strip of dough crosswise over the other dough strips, trimming any excess. Brush the bread stick with the beaten egg whites. Combine the remaining 2 teaspoons granulated sugar with the cinnamon and sprinkle over the bread stick. Press one end of the bread stick on top of the small end of dough strips for the handle of the rake.

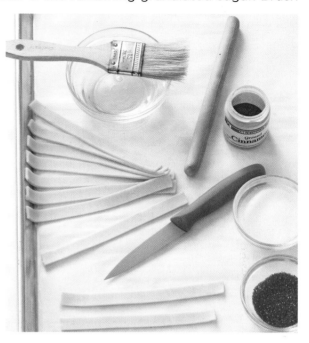

5 For the leaves, divide the remaining beaten egg whites among 4 small bowls. Tint each bowl a different bright color—red, green, yellow, and orange (using red and yellow)—with the food coloring. Roll out the remaining roll of dough on a lightly floured surface to a scant ¼-inch thickness. Using a variety of 2- to 3-inch leaf-shaped cookie cutters (see Sources), cut out leaf shapes, cutting as closely as possible. Transfer the shapes to the cookie sheets, about 1 inch apart.

6 Brush a quarter of the pie dough leaves with one of the tinted egg washes (see page 147). Use a toothpick to lightly score the veins in the leaves. Repeat with the remaining dough leaves and tinted egg washes, using a clean pastry brush for each color. Place some of the dough leaves against the rim of the cookie sheet to give them shape. Bake the dough leaves and rake in batches until just golden around the edges, 8 to 10 minutes. Transfer to a wire rack and cool completely.

7 Fold the fruit leather in half lengthwise. Wrap the fruit leather around the bread stick where it connects to the dough strips. Secure with a dot of water.

8 When ready to serve, arrange some of the leaves on top of the pie. Serve with the rake and extra leaves.

A PURITAN THANKSGIVING

NO-BAKE • MAKES ONE COUPLE; SERVES 20

Take the grim out of pilgrims by making them no-bake. Thanksgiving Puritans carved from store-bought pound cake are cloaked in candy-clay costumes with ice cream cone hats and shoes. Give thanks for the turkey, too.

2 recipes Candy Clay (page 230), one made with white chocolate chips and
    one made with semisweet chocolate chips
    Yellow and red food coloring
1 cup canned vanilla frosting
1 can (16 ounces) plus 1 cup dark chocolate frosting
5 wafer cup ice cream cones (Joy)
2 frozen pound cakes (16 ounces each; Sara Lee Family Size), thawed
3 marshmallows
3 jumbo yellow cupcakes or cranberry muffins
8 brown candy-coated chocolates (M&M's)

1 Line two cookie sheets with waxed paper. Tint ¼ cup of the white candy clay yellow with the food coloring. Working with one color of candy clay at a time, roll out the white, yellow, and chocolate clay between two sheets of waxed paper to a ⅛-inch thickness. Once all three colors have been rolled out separately, use the templates and a sharp knife to cut out the shapes indicated for each color (see pages 196 and 198). Cut a 2½-inch circle from the chocolate clay for the brim of the man's hat. Transfer the cut pieces to the cookie sheets. Reroll the clay scraps as needed. Shape 1 tablespoon of the chocolate clay into the 2-inch-long turkey head and neck. Use a toothpick to make the hole for the eye. Make a ¾-inch-long wattle with a small piece of the white clay. Cut a ½-inch triangle of yellow clay for the beak. Cover the shapes with plastic wrap to prevent drying.

2 Spoon 2 tablespoons of the vanilla frosting into a ziplock bag. Tint the remaining vanilla frosting very pale pink with the red food coloring. Spoon 1 tablespoon of the pink frosting into a ziplock bag. Spoon 2 tablespoons of the dark chocolate frosting into a ziplock bag. Press out the excess air and seal the bags. Cover the remaining pink frosting with plastic wrap to prevent drying.

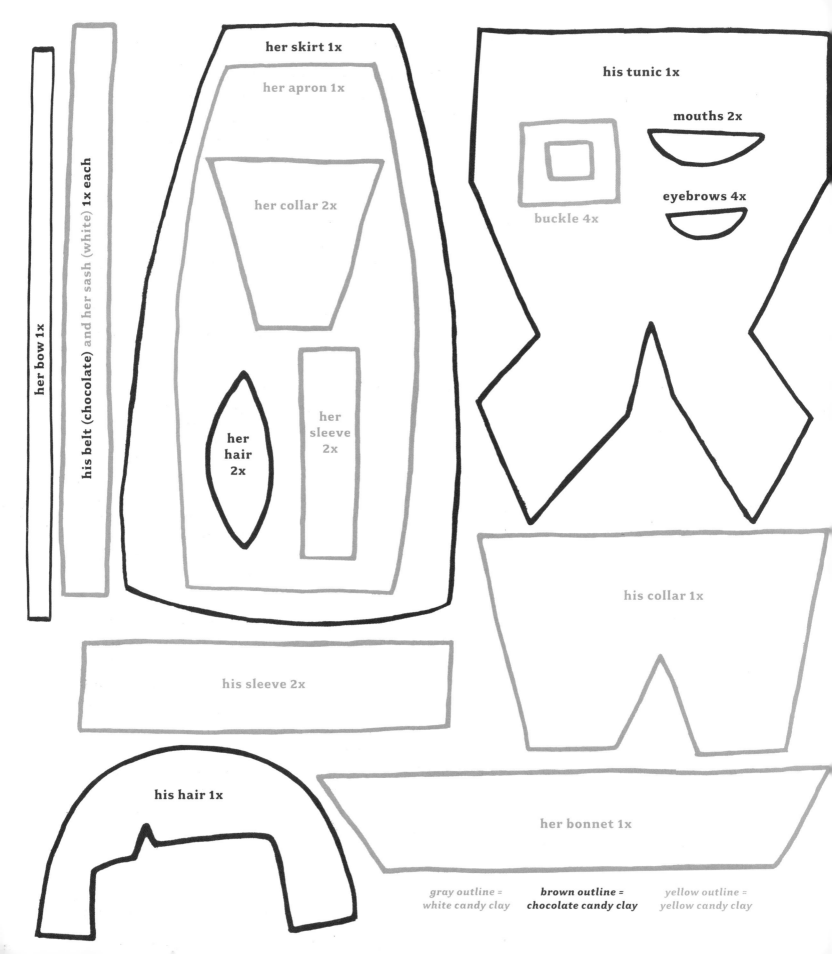

her bow 1x

his belt (chocolate) and her sash (white) **1x each**

her skirt 1x

her apron 1x

her collar 2x

her hair 2x

her sleeve 2x

his hair 1x

his sleeve 2x

her bonnet 1x

his tunic 1x

mouths 2x

eyebrows 4x

buckle 4x

his collar 1x

gray outline = white candy clay

brown outline = chocolate candy clay

yellow outline = yellow candy clay

3 Line a cookie sheet with waxed paper and place a wire rack on top. Microwave ½ cup of the dark chocolate frosting in a 1-cup glass measuring cup, stopping to stir frequently, until it has the texture of lightly whipped cream, 5 to 10 seconds. Dip the outside of each ice cream cone in the melted frosting to cover completely, allowing the excess frosting to drip back into the cup. Transfer the cones, open end down, to the wire rack. Refrigerate until set, about 30 minutes.

4 Place the pound cakes on a work surface with one short end facing you. For the man, using a small knife and starting at the end nearest you, remove a ½-by-5½-inch piece from each long side of the cake, to narrow the legs up to the waist. Make an angled cut to remove a piece on each side from the waist up to the top corner on the same side, to widen the shape at the shoulders. For the woman, starting at the top corner (the shoulders), make an angled cut to remove a piece on each side down to the waist, about 3½ inches down, coming in no more than ¾ inch at the waist. Round the corners from the waist out to the width of the cake to create the hips.

5 For the arms and shoes, cut 3 of the frosted ice cream cones in half lengthwise with a serrated knife. Cut 1 cone into quarters lengthwise. Place 4 of the cone halves on the work surface. Cut a 2-inch-long piece from the small end of 2 of the cones and a 1-inch-long piece from the small end of the other 2 cones for the shoes. Cut the marshmallows in half crosswise. Cut 2 halves in half again to make semicircles; you will have 4 halves and 4 quarters.

6 To assemble the pilgrims, snip a small (⅛-inch) corner from the bags with the frostings. Place the trimmed cakes on a serving platter about 4 inches apart. Spread the cakes with some of the remaining dark chocolate frosting to cover completely and smooth. Place the chocolate clay pieces for the man's tunic and belt and the woman's skirt on top of the frosted cakes, using the photo on page 195 as a guide. Place the white clay pieces for the woman's apron and sash and for the man's collar on top of the chocolate pieces. Place the woman's collar on the frosted cake. Use some vanilla frosting to attach the white clay sleeves: the man's sleeves go on the wide rim of the 2 halved cone pieces; the woman's sleeves go on the wide rim of 2 of the quartered pieces. For the hands, add a quartered piece of marshmallow behind each small sleeve and a half marshmallow behind each large sleeve, using some pink frosting to secure. Pipe on more of the pink frosting to cover the marshmallows. Arrange an arm on either side of the cakes, pressing into the frosting to secure (use the larger arms for the man). For the shoes, press 2 of the small cut pieces of cones, cut side down, into the bottom edge of each cake (use the larger pieces for the man). Spread some of the pink frosting on top of 2 of the cupcakes and smooth. Add the chocolate clay hair, eyebrows, and mouths and brown candy eyes. Pipe noses with the pink frosting.

7 To finish the man, pipe some of the chocolate frosting along the rim of the remaining whole cone and attach it to the chocolate clay brim. Attach a yellow buckle to the hat, belt, and each shoe with a dot of chocolate frosting. Add 3 brown candies for buttons, securing with dots of chocolate frosting.

8 To finish the woman, shape the chocolate clay strip into a bow and use a dot of chocolate frosting to attach it and secure the remaining brown candy. Add the white clay bonnet, short side up, on the outer edge of the cupcake, pressing lightly to secure. Pipe a decorative edge along the bonnet with the vanilla frosting. Add 2 halves and a quarter of a marshmallow to the platter above the bonnet.

9 For the turkey, spread the remaining chocolate frosting on top of the remaining cupcake and smooth. Use a fork to gently pull the frosting away from the center of the cupcake to make feather spikes all around. Add the 3 colored candy-clay tail feathers starting at the back edge of the cupcake with the largest piece. Add the candy-clay head and neck, wattle, and beak, using a dot of chocolate frosting to secure. Place the turkey cupcake on the platter between the Puritans.

turkey tail 1x

turkey tail 1x

turkey tail 1x

Big Tom

Is the tom on page 195 too teeny for your table? Supersize it by transforming the peacock (page 85) into a turkey fit for a crowd.

- **Make 3 batches of Candy Clay (page 230): white chocolate, semisweet chocolate, and butterscotch. Reserve a small portion of the white clay for the wattle. For the feathers, roll each flavor into a log and twist them together to make a braid (see photo, page 101). Roll out the braid ⅛ inch thick and cut it into 40 smooth-edged feathers 2½ inches long and 4 feathers 1½ inches long.**

- **Make an 8-inch round chocolate cake (from Perfect Cake Mix, page 224) and 13 chocolate cupcakes baked in white paper liners. Frost the cake and 12 of the cupcakes with 1 can (16 ounces) plus 1 cup chocolate frosting, spreading it from the center of the cake to look like feathers. For the head, tint ¼ cup canned vanilla frosting gray with black food coloring and frost the remaining cupcake with it. Arrange the 12 chocolate cupcakes around the cake for the body and add the gray cupcake to the top of the cake. Tint the reserved white candy clay red with food coloring and roll and shape it into the wattle. Attach the wattle to the head, using a thin pretzel stick for support. Starting on the back row, arrange the larger candy clay feathers on top of the chocolate cupcakes, overlapping slightly, to make a tail fan. Add the small feathers to the body in front of the head. Add a chocolate chip, flat side up, for the eye. Let the feast begin.**

GNOME SWEET GNOME

MAKES 12 GNOME-MADE SERVINGS

Gnomes have magical secrets, like how to turn Twizzlers and jelly beans into arms and hands and how to make a sparkling red hat from an ice cream cone coated in sugar. Watch how they magically make Christmas more fun.

- 12 sugar ice cream cones
- ¾ cup red decorating sugar (Cake Mate)
- ½ cup light corn syrup (Karo)
- 24 small yellow speckled and 36 small pink jelly beans (Jelly Belly)
- 12 blue licorice twists (Rainbow Twizzlers)
- 1 can (16 ounces) plus 1 cup vanilla frosting
  Neon blue, yellow, red, and green food coloring (McCormick)
- 12 mini yellow cupcakes
- 12 standard yellow cupcakes baked in blue paper liners (Reynolds)
- 24 mini chocolate chips (Nestlé)
- 6 large red spice drops
- 6 white spice drops
- 40 white candy decors (Cake Mate)
- ½ cup sweetened flaked coconut

1 Line a cookie sheet with waxed paper. Using a serrated knife, cut a 4-inch piece from the pointed end of each cone to make the hats. Place the red sugar in a shallow bowl. Microwave the corn syrup in a small bowl until bubbling, about 10 seconds. Brush the sides of one of the cones with a thin layer of the hot syrup and immediately roll it in the sugar to coat. Transfer the sugared cone to the cookie sheet, cut side down. Repeat with the remaining cones, reheating the syrup in the microwave for several seconds as necessary. For the arms and hands, dip one small end of 2 yellow jelly beans into the syrup and press one jelly bean into each open end of a blue licorice twist. Repeat with the remaining yellow candies to make 12 pairs of arms.

2 Tint 1 cup of the vanilla frosting neon blue with the food coloring. Tint ⅓ cup of the vanilla frosting light peach with the yellow and red food coloring. Cover the tinted frostings with plastic wrap to prevent drying. Divide the remaining vanilla frosting between 2 ziplock bags. Press out the excess air and seal the bags.

3 Trim the tops of the mini cupcakes level with a serrated knife and remove the paper liners. Spread the tops of the standard cupcakes with the blue frosting and smooth. Place a mini cupcake, trimmed side down, into the frosting on top of each standard cupcake, pressing to secure. Spread the peach frosting on one side of the mini cupcake for the face. To attach the arms, wrap the blue twists around the mini cupcake, jelly beans positioned to either side of the face area, and press into the blue frosting to secure.

4 Snip a small (⅛-inch) corner from the bags with the vanilla frosting. Working on one cupcake at a time, pipe vertical lines of vanilla frosting along the base of the mini cupcake for the hair and beard, always pulling the frosting down (leaving the peach-frosting face unpiped). Pipe overlapping rows to cover the back and sides of the mini cupcake, making the beard longer than the sides and back. To attach the hat, press a sugared cone on top of the cupcake.

For the mustache, pipe 2 horizontal lines of vanilla frosting above the beard. Attach the pink jelly beans for the nose and ears. Press the mini chocolate chips, flat side out, into the peach frosting for the eyes. Pipe horizontal eyebrows with the vanilla frosting. Repeat with the remaining cupcakes.

5 For the mushrooms, remove a small hole from the base of each large red spice drop with a small knife. Pinch the rounded end of each white spice drop to taper. Press the pointed end of a white spice drop into the base of a red spice drop to make the mushroom shape. Pipe small dots of vanilla frosting on top of the red spice drop and attach the white decors. Repeat with the remaining spice drops to make 6 mushrooms. For the grass, place the coconut in a ziplock bag. Add a few drops of green and yellow food coloring, seal the bag, and shake vigorously until the coconut is tinted green.

6 Place the gnomes on a serving platter. Decorate with the green coconut grass and spice drop mushrooms.

TICKY TACKY HOUSES

NO-BAKE • MAKES 7 HOUSES OF ONE COLOR; FOR A WHOLE HILLSIDE, MAKE A BATCH IN EACH COLOR

There's a pink one, and a blue one, and a green one, and a yellow one. And they're all made out of crispy rice cereal treats, and they all taste just the same. With Life Savers wreaths, these little houses on a hillside are the perfect holiday centerpiece and dessert.

INGREDIENTS FOR 7 HOUSES IN ONE COLOR
Nonstick cooking spray
2 **recipes Rice Cereal Treat (page 229)**
Red, blue, green, or yellow food coloring
1 each red and green fruit chews, plus your choice of 3 pink, blue, or yellow fruit chews
(AirHeads, Jolly Rancher, Laffy Taffy)
A selection of the following in a variety of colors for the roof tiles: fruit cereal O's (Froot Loops),
licorice twists (Rainbow Twizzlers), candy-coated chocolates (M&M's and Sixlets),
small jelly beans (Jelly Belly), sour belts and straws, licorice pastels (Jelly Belly),
tube-shaped candies (Mike and Ike)
½ **recipe Royal Frosting (page 232)**
Red and green O-shaped hard candies (Life Savers)
Pearl sprinkles (Wilton)
Sweetened flaked coconut (optional)

1 Grease a 9-by-13-inch cake pan with nonstick cooking spray. Tint the rice cereal treat using the red, blue, green, or yellow food coloring.

2 With well-greased hands, press the tinted cereal mixture into half of the pan, pressing the mixture firmly, to make a 9-by-6½-inch rectangle. Use the bottom of a greased measuring cup to make the exposed side and top straight. Allow the treat to set for 30 minutes.

3 Line a cookie sheet with waxed paper. Microwave the 5 fruit chews for no more than 3 seconds to soften. Roll out each chew to a ⅛-inch thickness. For the ribbons on the candy wreaths, cut the red and green fruit chews into ½-inch triangles; you'll need 7 triangles. Make a cut almost all the way from the base to the opposite point of each triangle for the ribbon tails. Cut a small notch from each tail end. For the doors, cut the remaining 3 chews into 1¼-by-¾-inch rectangles, rerolling the scraps as necessary to make 7 pieces. For the roof tiles, cut the large candies, like licorice twists, sour belts, and straws, into 1-inch pieces.

4 Place the firm rice cereal treat on a work surface. Using the template above and a serrated knife, cut the treat into 6 whole shapes and 2 half shapes, pressing the 2 halves together to make the 7th house (see photo).

5 Place the royal frosting in a ziplock bag. Press out the excess air and seal the bag. Snip a small (⅛-inch) corner from the bag. Working on one house at a time, pipe some of the royal frosting along the lower edge of the roof. Attach the desired roof tile candies in a row, pressing into the frosting to secure. Pipe another line of frosting above the candies and attach another row of roof tiles, overlapping slightly. Continue to cover both sides of the roof. Repeat with the remaining houses and candies of your choice.

6 Pipe dots of frosting on the front of one of the houses and attach the door, a candy-O wreath, a ribbon, and a pearl sprinkle for the doorknob. Pipe icicles with the frosting along the roofline using the squeeze-release-pull technique (see page 75). Repeat with the remaining houses. Allow the houses to dry for at least 1 hour.

7 Arrange the houses on a serving platter. For the snow, sprinkle the platter with the chopped coconut, if desired.

HANG IN THERE, COOKIE

There's nothing cookie cutter about cookie hangers. Create a notch big enough to fit on the rim of a coffee cup, pudding bowl, or milk glass, and you have a well-balanced dessert.

BASIC COOKIE HANGER

Follow the directions for Quick Sugar Cookie Dough (page 226; any flavor dough) through step 2. Cut out the cookies using the cookie cutter (or a small knife) specified for the following recipes. Transfer the dough shapes to the cookie sheets. Use a small knife to cut a ¾-by-¼-inch notch from one side (check the thickness of the cup or glass you are going to use and adjust the cut notch accordingly, making it slightly larger than the cup). Repeat with the remaining dough and scraps. Continue with step 3 to bake the cookies. After decorating, let the cookies dry for at least 1 hour. Wait until just before serving to add the cookie hanger to the lip of the cup or glass, and if serving with a liquid, underfill to keep the hanger dry.

GINGERBREAD BOYS

MAKES 8 TO 10 (3½-INCH) COOKIES

½ **recipe Quick Spice Cookie Dough (page 227)**
1 **3½-inch gingerbread-boy cookie cutter (see Sources)**
½ **recipe Royal Frosting (page 232)**
 Red and black food coloring (McCormick)
 Red and green mini candy-coated chocolates (M&M's Minis)

1 Follow the Basic Cookie Hanger directions above, using the spice cookie dough and ginger-bread boy cookie cutter.

2 Tint 3 tablespoons of the royal frosting red and 3 tablespoons black using the food coloring. Spoon each color plus the remaining royal frosting into separate ziplock bags. Press out the excess air and seal the bags. Snip a small (⅛-inch) corner from the bags. Pipe wavy lines of white frosting on the arms and legs of each cookie and attach the red and green candy as buttons with dots of white frosting. Pipe black eyes and a red mouth with the tinted frostings.

SNOWFLAKES

MAKES 8 TO 10 (3½-INCH) COOKIES

½ recipe Quick Chocolate Cookie Dough (page 227)
1 3½-inch snowflake cookie cutter (see Sources)
½ recipe Royal Frosting (page 232)
½ cup white decorating sugar (see Sources)

1 Follow the Basic Cookie Hanger directions (page 206), using the chocolate cookie dough and snowflake cookie cutter.

2 Spoon the royal frosting into a ziplock bag. Press out the excess air and seal the bag. Snip a small (⅛-inch) corner from the bag. Pipe decorative swirls, lines, or dots of frosting on top of each cookie. While the frosting is still wet, sprinkle the top of the cookie with the sugar to cover. Shake off any excess sugar.

DOUGHNUT COOKIES

MAKES 16 TO 20 (3½-INCH) COOKIES

½ **recipe Quick Spice Cookie Dough (page 227)**
½ **recipe Quick Chocolate Cookie Dough (page 227)**
1 **3-inch and one 1-inch round cookie cutter (see Sources)**
½ **recipe Royal Frosting (page 232)**
　 Red food coloring
3 **tablespoons rainbow sprinkles**

1 Follow the Basic Cookie Hanger directions (page 206), using the spice cookie dough and chocolate cookie dough and a 3-inch round cutter. Before baking, remove a 1-inch circle from the center of each cookie.

2 Tint half of the royal frosting pink with the food coloring. Add a few drops of water to the pink and white royal frosting to thin slightly; it will have the texture of lightly whipped cream. Spread some of either color frosting on top of each cookie, giving it a scalloped edge. While the frosting is still wet, sprinkle the tops of the cookies with the rainbow sprinkles.

TEA FOR TWO

MAKES 8 TO 10 (3½-INCH) COOKIES

½ recipe Quick Spice Cookie Dough (page 227)
4 black licorice laces (see Sources)
¼ cup red decorating sugar (Cake Mate)
12 red spice drops
½ recipe Royal Frosting (page 232)

1 Follow the Basic Cookie Hanger directions (page 206), using the spice cookie dough. Using a small knife, cut out an equal number of 2-by-2½-inch rectangles and 1¼-inch squares. Transfer the dough pieces to the pans. Make a ½-inch diagonal cut from two corners of one short side of each rectangle to make a tea-bag shape. Before baking, press a 3-inch piece of black licorice lace into the dough at the top of the tapered end of the tea bag. Press the other end of the licorice lace into a small dough square. Continue with the basic directions for baking.

2 Sprinkle the work surface with the red sugar. Roll out the spice drops in the red sugar until flattened. Cut each piece into a 1¼-inch square.

3 Spoon half of the royal frosting into a ziplock bag. Press out the excess air and seal the bag. Add a few drops of water to the remaining royal frosting to thin slightly; it will have the texture of lightly whipped cream. Spread some of the thinned frosting on the top half of the larger cookie. Snip a small (⅛-inch) corner from the bag with the frosting. Pipe a frosting outline on the larger cookie. Attach the spice drop square to the smaller cookie with a few dots of the frosting and pipe T42 or T4U on top. Repeat with the remaining cookies, frosting, and spice drops.

well-balanced

THE LIGHTING OF THE TREE

LIGHTS 1 TREE; MAKES 24 CUPCAKES

Easy to make and fun to use, candy clay turns this cupcake Christmas tree into a stunning centerpiece for your celebration. String the lights with candy-coated sunflower seeds.

2	recipes Candy Clay (page 230), made with white chocolate chips
	Yellow and green food coloring
1	can (16 ounces) plus ½ cup vanilla frosting
3	tablespoons yellow decorating sugar (Cake Mate)
24	vanilla cupcakes baked in green foil liners (Reynolds)
4	chocolate-covered cookie sticks (Kit Kat)
¼	cup assorted candy-coated chocolate-covered sunflower seeds (Sunny Seed Drops)

1 Tint 2 tablespoons of the candy clay bright yellow with the yellow food coloring (see page 89). Divide the remaining candy clay in half. Tint half of the clay light green with the green and yellow food coloring. Tint the remaining half bright green with the green food coloring. Knead each piece of candy clay until smooth and the color is well blended. Cover the clay with plastic wrap to prevent drying.

2 Line two cookie sheets with waxed paper. Roll out the yellow candy clay between two sheets of waxed paper ⅛ inch thick. Using a 2½-inch star-shaped cookie cutter or a small knife, cut out a yellow star. Transfer to a cookie sheet and cover with plastic wrap to prevent it from drying. Roll half of the bright green clay between two sheets of waxed paper to

a ⅛-inch thickness. Using a 2¾-inch round cookie cutter or the rim of a small glass, cut the candy clay into circles. Trim each circle with a paring knife or a strip of brass (see Sources) shaped into a zigzag, to remove about one third of the circle. Transfer the larger shapes to the pans and keep covered with plastic wrap to prevent drying out. Combine the scraps and trimmings with the other half of the bright green clay and repeat to make 21 pieces. Repeat with the light green candy clay, but this time trim away a little less than half of the circle to create 21 slightly smaller pieces (see photo).

3 Tint ¼ cup of the vanilla frosting yellow-green with the food coloring. Spoon the frosting into a ziplock bag, press out the excess air, and seal the bag. Spoon the yellow sugar into a shallow bowl. Spread the tops of 3 of the cupcakes with some of the remaining vanilla frosting and smooth. Roll the edge of one of the frosted cupcakes in the yellow sugar. Tint the remaining vanilla frosting bright green with the green food coloring. Spread the bright green frosting on top of the remaining 21 cupcakes and smooth.

4 Arrange the cupcakes on a large serving platter, placing the sugared white cupcake at the top. Place 1 green cupcake below the sugared cupcake followed by the remaining green cupcakes in rows of 2, 3, 4, 5, and 6, (see photo, page 212). Arrange the 2 remaining vanilla-frosted cupcakes in the center below the last row of green cupcakes.

5 Place a bright green candy-clay piece on the lower half of each green-frosted cupcake. Add a lighter green candy-clay piece, slightly overlapping the darker green piece and covering the top edge of the cupcake, pressing into the frosting to secure. Place the yellow star on the top cupcake. For the trunk, add the chocolate-covered cookie sticks, vertically, on the bottom 2 vanilla-frosted cupcakes.

6 Snip a very small (¹⁄₁₆-inch) corner from the bag with the yellow-green frosting. For the string of lights, pipe lines of frosting over the bright green candy clay. Add the candy-coated sunflower seeds for the lights. Pipe a dot of frosting at the top of each piece of candy for the light socket.

string the lights

STOCKING STUFFERS

MAKES 7 CHRISTMAS STOCKINGS

Sock-shaped pastries to hang by the chimney with care come already stuffed—with cherry pie filling. Each stocking is painted with a colorful egg wash and baked to crispy perfection.

> 4 rolls (2 boxes; 14.1 ounces each) refrigerated pie dough (Pillsbury)
> All-purpose flour
> 2 cans (21 ounces each) cherry pie filling, lightly drained
> 2 large egg whites, lightly beaten
> Red, green, yellow, and blue food coloring
> ½ cup white candy melting wafers (Wilton)
> ½ cup mini candy-covered chocolates (M&M's Minis)

1 Preheat the oven to 375°F. Line two cookie sheets with parchment paper. Unroll 1 refrigerated pie dough on a lightly floured surface. Roll out to an 11-inch circle. Use the templates on page 217 to cut out as many stocking shapes as possible. Repeat with the remaining dough to make 14 pieces (7 large and 7 small).

2 Place 3 or 4 of the smaller pieces of dough on each cookie sheet. Spoon some of the drained cherry pie filling down the center of each piece (see photo). Brush the outer edge of the dough with some of the egg whites. Place a larger dough piece on top of the piece with the filling, gently draping it over the filling, lining up the edges, and pressing together. Use the tines of a fork to seal the edges of the dough and make a decorative edge.

3 Divide the remaining egg whites among 4 small bowls. Tint each bowl a different color using the red, green, yellow, and blue food coloring. Using a separate small pastry or craft brush for each color, paint decorative patterns on the tops of the dough with the colored egg whites, leaving ⅛ inch between each color. For a darker color, refrigerate for 10 minutes, then paint a second coat of the same color on top.

4 Bake, rotating the pans halfway through baking, until the stockings are lightly golden and
    cooked through, about 15 minutes. Transfer to a wire rack to cool.

5 Place the white candy melts in a ziplock bag (do not seal the bag). Microwave for 10 seconds
    to soften. Massage the candy, return to the microwave, and repeat the process until the
    candy is smooth, about 40 seconds. Press out the excess air and seal the bag. Snip a small
    (⅛-inch) corner from the bag. Pipe decorative lines and dots on top of the cooled stockings.
    Attach some of the chocolate candies to the dots to make desired patterns.

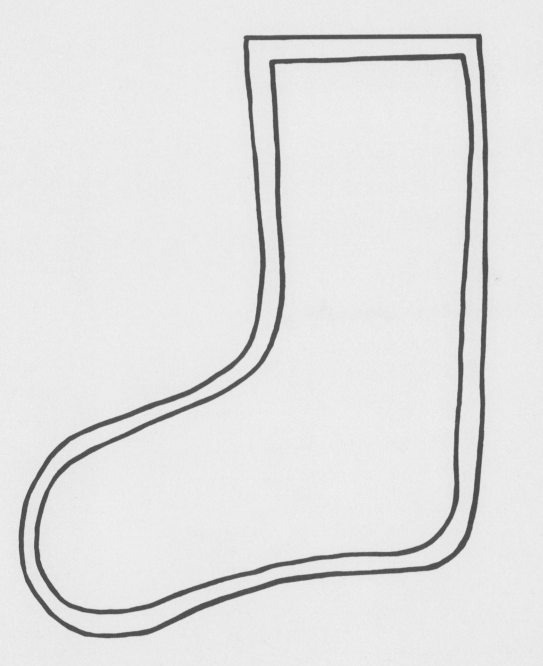

WHITEOUT CAKE

MAKES 1 CAKE; SERVES 20

A blizzard of marshmallow petals coated in glittering white sugar and dotted with pearlized candies makes this layer cake a spectacular finish to a holiday meal. And because the flowers can be made ahead of time, it is also a perfect DIY wedding cake.

- 1 **cup white decorating sugar (see Sources)**
- 12 **marshmallows**
- 125 **mini marshmallows (one 10.5-ounce bag)**
- 1 **cup white candy melting wafers (Wilton)**
- 2 **recipes Almost-Homemade Vanilla Buttercream (page 231)**
- 1 **recipe Perfect Cake Mix (page 224), made with devil's food cake, baked in two 8-inch round and one 5½-inch round pans (see Sources)**
- 86 **white candy pearls (see Sources)**

1 For the flowers, place the white decorating sugar in a medium bowl. Make the petals for the large flowers by cutting the large marshmallows crosswise into 5 thin slices, allowing the pieces to fall into the sugar. Shake the bowl and press the cut sides of the marshmallows into the sugar to coat. Make the petals for the small flowers by cutting the mini marshmallows in half on the diagonal, then coat in sugar as above. Remove the sugared marshmallow petals and store in an airtight container.

2 Line three cookie sheets with waxed paper. Place the white candy melts in a ziplock bag (do not seal the bag). Microwave for 10 seconds to soften, massage the wafers in the bag, return to the microwave, and repeat the process until smooth, about 30 seconds. Press out the excess air and seal the bag. Snip a small (⅛-inch) corner from the bag. For the large flowers, pipe a dot of melted candy about the size of a dime onto the waxed paper and arrange 5 large marshmallow slices, sugared side up, in the shape of a flower in the dot of melted candy (see photo). Repeat to make 12 flowers. Refrigerate for 5 minutes, or until the candy is set. For the small flowers, pipe a dot of melted candy the size of a bean onto the waxed paper. Arrange 5 mini marshmallow pieces, sugared side up, in the shape of a flower on top of the melted candy. Repeat to make 50 flowers. Refrigerate for 5 minutes, or until the candy is set. (The flowers can be made up to this point and stored in an airtight container for up to 1 week.)

3 Spoon ¼ cup of the vanilla frosting into a ziplock bag. Place one 8-inch cake layer on a work surface. Use toothpicks around the outer edge of the cake to mark the cake into 3 layers. Cut the cake horizontally into layers with a serrated knife, using the toothpicks as a guide. Repeat with the other 8-inch cake. Cut the smaller cake into 4 layers.

4 Transfer one 8-inch cake layer to a serving platter. Spread a scant ⅓ cup of the remaining vanilla frosting on top of the cake. Place another layer on top and repeat the process 4 times, ending with frosting, to make 6 layers. Spread a thin coating of vanilla frosting on the side of the cake to smooth. Place a 5½-inch cake layer on a serving plate. Spread a scant ¼ cup vanilla frosting on top. Place another layer of cake on top and repeat the process 2 times, ending with frosting, to make 4 layers. Spread a thin coating of vanilla frosting on the side of the cake to smooth and fill any gaps. Refrigerate both cakes until set, about 1 hour.

5 Place the small cake on top of the large cake. Spread the remaining vanilla frosting on top of the cake and smooth. Snip a small corner from the bag with the vanilla frosting. Carefully peel the large and small flowers from the waxed paper. Arrange the flowers as desired on the top and sides of the cake, adding some vanilla frosting, if necessary, to secure. Pipe small dots of vanilla frosting in the center of the flowers and add the pearl candies, using 3 for each large flower and 1 for each small flower.

master recipes

Off-the-shelf doesn't have to mean ordinary: our recipes just leave you with more time to decorate. With a few adjustments, cake, cookie, and brownie mixes become perfect canvases for decorating. Because you can mold them into any shape, we have added rice cereal treats to our repertoire, too. If your design calls for big sheets of candy in a wide range of colors, candy clay is the way to go. Easy to make, it doesn't wilt in high humidity.

As for frosting, canned is essential for dipping or pouring (homemade won't firm back up after being heated). For a special occasion when the frosting does not need to be heated, Almost-Homemade Buttercream is silky smooth and delicious and forms perfect peaks. For a more resilient frosting, try Royal Frosting, especially for cookie projects.

PERFECT CAKE MIX

With the addition of buttermilk and an extra egg, our doctored cake mix makes a cake that tastes great and is firm enough for all of your cupcake and cake designs.

Nonstick cooking spray
1 box (18.25 ounces) cake mix (such as classic vanilla, yellow, or devil's food)
1 cup buttermilk (in place of the water called for on the box)
Vegetable oil (the amount called for on the box)
4 large eggs (in place of the number called for on the box)

1 Preheat the oven to 350°F. Line muffin cups with paper liners or line the bottom of the pan(s) with waxed paper to fit and spray with nonstick cooking spray.

2 Following the box's instructions, combine all the ingredients in a large bowl: use the buttermilk in place of the water specified (the box will call for more water than the buttermilk here), use the amount of oil called for on the box (typically, white or yellow cake calls for ⅓ cup; chocolate cakes call for ½ cup), and add the 4 eggs. Beat with an electric mixer on low speed until moistened, about 30 seconds. Increase the mixer speed to high and beat until thick, 2 minutes longer.

3 Using the chart on the opposite page, divide the batter between the pans, smooth the top(s), and follow the indicated baking times. Bake until golden and a toothpick inserted in the center comes out clean.

4 Transfer the cake(s) to a wire rack and cool for 15 minutes. Invert, lift off the pan(s), and cool completely.

5 Cakes or cupcakes that are not used immediately may be wrapped in plastic wrap and frozen for up to 2 weeks.

VESSEL	AMOUNT	YIELD	TIME
jumbo cupcake pan	evenly divided	12	20 to 25 min
popover pan	evenly divided	16	18 to 22 min
standard cupcake pan	evenly divided	24	15 to 20 min
mini cupcake pan	evenly divided	48	8 to 12 min
one 10-by-2-inch deep round pan	full recipe	1	35 to 40 min
two 9-inch round or square pans	evenly divided	2	28 to 30 min
two 8-inch round or square pans	evenly divided	2	32 to 35 min
one 9-by-13-inch pan	full recipe	1	32 to 38 min
1½-quart oven-safe glass bowl	full recipe	1	40 to 50 min
+ one 5½-inch round	1½ cups	1	20 to 22 min
two 8-inch round pans	remainder evenly divided	2	20 to 22 min
+ 12 standard cupcakes	two-thirds full	12	15 to 20 min
one 8-inch round pan	remaining batter	1	30 to 35 min
+ 5 standard cupcakes	two-thirds full	5	15 to 20 min
one 10½-by-15½-inch jelly-roll pan	remaining batter	1	15 to 20 min
+ one 2-cup oven-safe glass measuring cup	1 cup	1	18 to 25 min
16 standard cupcakes	remainder evenly divided	16	15 to 20 min

QUICK SUGAR COOKIE DOUGH

MAKES 16 TO 20 (3-INCH) COOKIES

We doctor store-bought sugar cookie dough so it's easier to handle and is ready to be used right away. It tastes great, too.

⅔ **cup all-purpose flour, plus extra for rolling**
1 **tube (16.5 ounces) refrigerated sugar cookie dough**

1 Preheat the oven to 350°F. Line two cookie sheets with parchment paper. Knead the flour into the dough until smooth. Divide the dough in half. Roll out each piece on a lightly floured surface to a scant ¼-inch thickness.

2 Cut out the desired shapes according to the recipe, using templates or a cookie cutter and cutting as close together as possible. Transfer the shapes to the cookie sheets, spacing about 1 inch apart. Remove any areas of the cookies if directed in the recipe.

3 Bake until golden and firm to the touch, 7 to 12 minutes depending on the size and shape of the cookies. Transfer to a wire rack and cool completely.

QUICK LEMON COOKIE DOUGH

2/3 cup all-purpose flour, plus extra for rolling
1 tube (16.5 ounces) refrigerated sugar cookie dough
1 teaspoon lemon zest

Make as directed, kneading in the lemon zest with the flour until well blended.

QUICK SPICE COOKIE DOUGH

2/3 cup all-purpose flour, plus extra for rolling
1 tube (16.5 ounces) refrigerated sugar cookie dough
1 teaspoon apple pie spice

Make as directed, kneading in the apple pie spice with the flour until well blended.

GRAHAM CRACKER COOKIE DOUGH

1/4 cup all-purpose flour, plus extra for rolling
1 tube (16.5 ounces) refrigerated sugar cookie dough
1/2 cup graham cracker crumbs

Make as directed, kneading in the graham cracker crumbs with the flour until well blended.

QUICK CHOCOLATE COOKIE DOUGH

1/4 cup all-purpose flour, plus extra for rolling
1 tube (16.5 ounces) refrigerated sugar cookie dough
1/3 cup unsweetened cocoa powder

Make as directed, kneading in the cocoa powder with the flour until well blended.

PERFECT BROWNIE MIX

MAKES 16 BROWNIES

Store-bought brownie mix can sometimes be too soft for decorating. Our doctored version makes a firm, cakelike brownie that is project-perfect.

Nonstick cooking spray
1 box (19.9 ounces) chewy fudge brownie mix
½ cup buttermilk (in place of the water called for on the box)
½ cup vegetable oil
3 large eggs (in place of the number called for on the box)

1 Preheat the oven to 350°F. Line a 9-by-13-inch or a 10-inch round baking pan (see Sources) with foil, allowing the foil to hang over the edges. Spray the pan and foil with nonstick cooking spray. Following the box's instructions, combine all the ingredients in a large bowl. Use the buttermilk in place of the water specified (the box will call for less water than the buttermilk here), ½ cup oil, and the 3 eggs to make a cakelike brownie. Stir until just combined (about 50 strokes).

2 Spread the batter in the prepared pan and smooth. Bake until puffed and a toothpick inserted in the center comes out clean, 27 to 30 minutes. Transfer to a wire rack. Cool completely in the pan before removing and cutting the brownies.

RICE CEREAL TREAT

MAKES ABOUT 3 CUPS

Rice cereal treats are great because you can shape them any way you want (see photos, page 106).

    2½ cups mini marshmallows
    2   tablespoons butter
        Food coloring (optional)
    3   cups rice cereal (Rice Krispies)
        Nonstick cooking spray

1 Place the mini marshmallows and butter in a large bowl and microwave on high until melted, about 1½ minutes. Stir until smooth. For a tinted treat, add the desired food coloring at this point.

2 Fold in the rice cereal until well blended.

3 Spray your clean hands and cake pan, if using, liberally with the nonstick cooking spray and follow the recipe to shape as desired.

CHOCOLATE RICE CEREAL TREAT

MAKES ABOUT 3 CUPS

    ½   cup mini chocolate chips (Nestlé)
    2½ cups mini marshmallows
    2   tablespoons butter
    3   cups rice cereal (Rice Krispies)
        Nonstick cooking spray

Make as directed, adding the mini chocolate chips to the marshmallows and butter before melting. Follow the recipe to shape as desired.

CANDY CLAY

MAKES ABOUT 1¼ CUPS

Candy clay works like colored taffy or fondant and can be tinted, rolled, shaped, and textured (see photos, page 89).

> **1 bag (12 ounces) white chocolate, semisweet chocolate, or butterscotch chips (Nestlé or Ghirardelli) or 1 bag (14 ounces) candy melts, any color (Wilton)**
> **⅓ cup light corn syrup (Karo)**
> **Food coloring (optional)**

1 Place the chips in a medium glass bowl. Microwave on high, stopping to stir every 20 seconds, until the candy is melted and smooth, about 1 minute (it is important not to overheat).

2 Add the corn syrup and stir with a rubber spatula until well combined. The mixture will look grainy. Cover the clay tightly with plastic wrap and let stand at room temperature for at least 3 hours to firm up. The candy clay can be made up to 4 days in advance and stored, covered, at room temperature.

3 When ready to use, knead the clay until smooth. (If the candy clay was made several days in advance and is too firm, microwave the clay for 5 to 10 seconds to soften.)

4 Tint the white chocolate candy clay with the food coloring, if desired, kneading the clay well to blend the color. Divide the candy clay into smaller pieces. Roll out each piece between two sheets of waxed paper to a ⅛-inch or thinner thickness. Cut the clay into the desired shapes with a cookie cutter, small knife, or clean scissors. To make shapes, work the candy clay like modeling clay. Place the shapes on a waxed paper–lined cookie sheet and cover with plastic wrap to prevent drying. Follow the directions for use of candy clay in each recipe.

ALMOST-HOMEMADE VANILLA BUTTERCREAM

MAKES ABOUT 3½ CUPS

This silky-textured frosting is similar to French buttercream.

> 3 sticks (¾ pound) unsalted butter, softened and cut into 1-inch pieces
> 1 container (16 ounces) marshmallow creme (Marshmallow Fluff)
> ½ cup confectioners' sugar, plus more if desired
> 1 teaspoon vanilla extract
> Food coloring (optional)

1 In a large mixing bowl, beat the butter with an electric mixer on medium speed until light and fluffy. Add the marshmallow creme and beat until smooth, scraping down the sides of the bowl. Add the confectioners' sugar and vanilla extract and beat until light and fluffy. If the mixture seems too stiff, soften in the microwave for no more than 10 seconds and beat again until smooth.

2 Taste, and add up to 1 cup more confectioners' sugar, if desired, for sweetness (the frosting may be tinted at this time).

ALMOST-HOMEMADE COCOA BUTTERCREAM

MAKES ABOUT 3½ CUPS

This cocoa buttercream is not dark chocolate in color. For darker designs, we use dark chocolate canned frosting.

> 1 recipe Almost-Homemade Vanilla Buttercream
> 3 tablespoons unsweetened cocoa powder

Follow the directions for the vanilla buttercream, adding the cocoa powder with the confectioners' sugar and leaving out the food coloring. Beat well to combine.

ROYAL FROSTING

MAKES ABOUT 2 CUPS

Although it takes time to dry, this frosting is great for details and colorful decorations because it is tough enough to stand up to travel.

  1 box (16 ounces) confectioners' sugar
  3 tablespoons powdered egg whites (Just Whites)
  6 tablespoons warm water
     Food coloring (optional)

Combine all the ingredients in a medium bowl. Beat with an electric mixer on low speed until blended. Increase the speed to high and beat until smooth and thick (the frosting may be tinted at this time). Use as directed in the recipe.

essential tools

Our favorite cupcaking tools are so ordinary, you probably already have them somewhere in your house. Put them together in one spot, and you've got a decorating pantry.

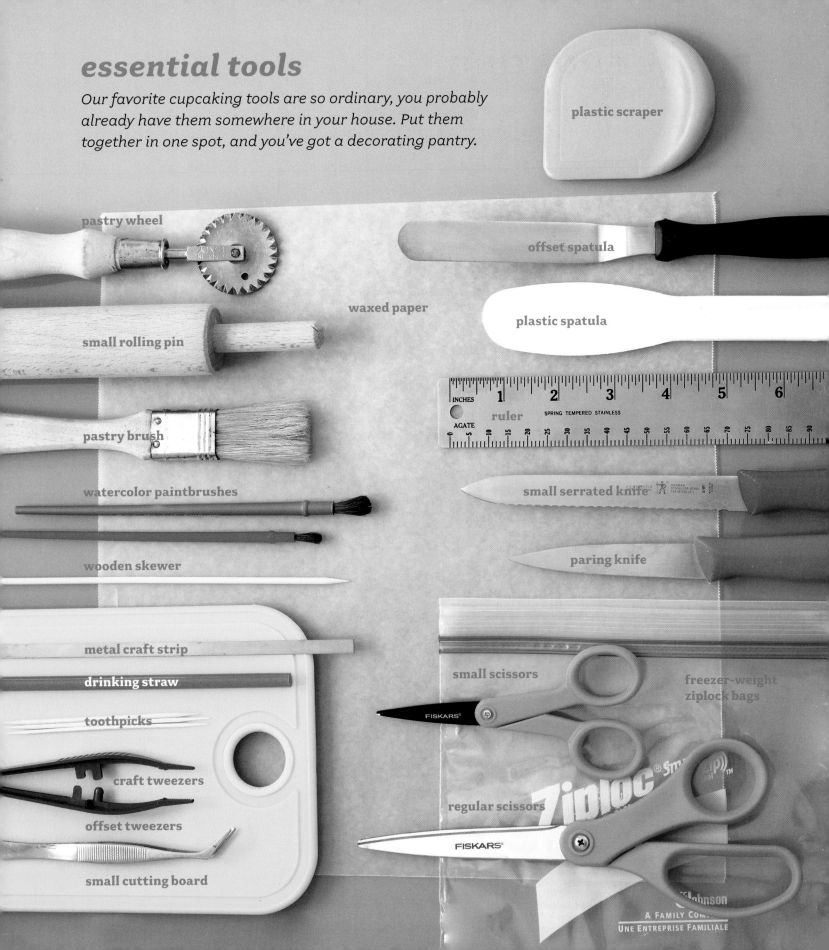

plastic scraper

pastry wheel

offset spatula

waxed paper

plastic spatula

small rolling pin

ruler

INCHES 1 2 3 4 5 6
AGATE
SPRING TEMPERED STAINLESS

pastry brush

small serrated knife

watercolor paintbrushes

paring knife

wooden skewer

metal craft strip

small scissors

freezer-weight ziplock bags

drinking straw

toothpicks

FISKARS

craft tweezers

regular scissors

Ziploc® SmartZip™

offset tweezers

FISKARS

small cutting board

c.Johnson

A FAMILY COMP
UNE ENTREPRISE FAMILIALE

SOURCES

BAKING SUPPLIES

ATECO
(800) 645-7170
www.atecousa.net

Offset spatulas. A good source for cake decorating tools.

BERYL'S
P.O. Box 1584
North Springfield, VA 22151
(703) 256-6951
(800) 488-2749
www.beryls.com

A wide variety of cupcake paper liners, as well as many other cupcake decorating supplies.

CAKE MATE
www.cakemate.com

A complete list of sugar and sprinkles available at your local grocery store, as well as creative cupcake ideas.

CONFECTIONERY HOUSE
(518) 279-4250
www.confectioneryhouse.com

Solid-color (including gold and black) cupcake paper liners in three sizes. A wide variety of candy melting wafers, sprinkles, food coloring, and luster dust.

COUNTRY KITCHEN SWEETART
4621 Speedway Drive
Fort Wayne, IN 46825
(260) 482-4835
(800) 497-3927
www.countrykitchensa.com

Sanding and coarse sugars. A wide variety of candy decors, sprinkles, luster dust, candy melting wafers, food coloring, and paper liners.

DOWNTOWN DOUGH
W63 N658 Washington Avenue
Cedarburg, WI 53012
(262) 387-0311
www.downtowndough.com

A great source for cookie cutters: gingerbread boys and girls, sun, snowflakes, circles—over 1,600 from which to choose, plus a huge selection of sprinkles and decorations.

DUNCAN HINES
www.duncanhines.com

A complete list of cake mixes and frostings available at your local grocery store, as well as creative cupcake ideas and tips and ideas for baking.

FANCY FLOURS
www.fancyflours.com

Beautiful and elegant cupcake supplies, from paper liners to specialty sugars, sprinkles, and decorations.

INDIA TREE GOURMET SPICES & SPECIALTIES
1435 Elliott Avenue West
Seattle, WA 98119
(206) 286-9988
(800) 596-0885
www.indiatree.com

Beautiful coarse sugars and decorating sugars. India Tree products are also available in some grocery stores.

KITCHEN KRAFTS
P.O. Box 442
Waukon, IA 52172
(563) 535-8000
(800) 298-5389
www.kitchenkrafts.com

A wide variety of decorating supplies.

McCORMICK
www.mccormick.com

A great source for large-sized food coloring and hard-to-find colors like neon and black and a strong selection of seasonal cupcake ideas. The color wheel on the food-color section of the site makes it easy to create custom colors.

N.Y. CAKE & BAKING DIST.
56 West 22nd Street
New York, NY 10010
(212) 675-2253
(800) 942-2539

N.Y. Cake West
10665 W. Pico Boulevard
Los Angeles, CA 90064
(310) 481-0875
(877) NYCAKE-8
www.nycake.com

Food coloring, candy melting wafers, luster dust, dragées, sugars, sprinkles, and some paper liners.

SUGARCRAFT
3665 Dixie Highway
Hamilton, OH 45015
(513) 896-7089
www.sugarcraft.com

A wide variety of baking and decorating supplies.

SUR LA TABLE
(800) 243-0852
www.surlatable.com

Crinkle cutters, pastry wheels, bakeware, tiered cake stands. Schedules of decorating classes at stores.

WILLIAMS-SONOMA
www.williams-sonoma.com

Cake plates, mini pie plates, platters, sprinkles, and other baking equipment.

WILTON INDUSTRIES
2240 West 75th Street
Woodridge, IL 60517
(630) 963-1818
(800) 794-5866
www.wilton.com

A wide variety of baking supplies, including candy melting wafers, food coloring, paper liners, assorted sprinkles and sugars, white candy pearls, and much more. Wilton products are also available in many craft and party stores and some grocery stores.

PARTY AND CRAFT SUPPLIES

A.C. MOORE
www.acmoore.com

Marvy paper punch, plastic eggs, cake decorating supplies and crafts, as well as books. Store locations are listed online.

BEADALON
www.beadalon.com

Offset tweezers. A great source for sorting trays and crafting mats.

FISKARS
www.fiskars.com

Small, regular, and craft scissors, creative craft ideas, seminars, and products.

FRESHPRESERVINGSTORE.COM
A variety of different glass canning jars.

MICHAELS STORES
(800) 642-4235
www.michaels.com

Marvy paper punch, plastic eggs, a wide variety of craft supplies and cake decorating supplies, including Wilton products.

PAPER SOURCE
www.paper-source.com

Beautiful papers and crafting supplies (including flexible patterned or solid-color paper), packing material, and boxes for cupcake gifts.

PARTY CITY
www.partycity.com

Large variety of colored plastic forks, paper napkins, and plates. Candies in bulk.

REYNOLDS
www.reynoldskitchens.com

The latest seasonal paper and foil liner selections, as well as creative cupcake ideas.

TOWER HOBBIES SUPPLIES
(217) 398-3636
(800) 637-6050
www.towerhobbies.com

Thin brass strips for making cookie cutters; carries K&S brass supplies.

OTHER CRAFT SUPPLIES

HEFTY
heftybrands.pactiv.com

Product information on food storage bags as well as promotions and coupons.

ZIPLOC
www.ziploc.com

Product information, as well as coupons for Ziploc products.

GOURMET CANDY SUPPLIES

BALBOA CANDY
301-J Marine Street
Newport Beach, CA 92662
(949) 723-6099
www.balboacandy.com

A great candy selection, specializing in retro candies and taffy.

DYLAN'S CANDY BAR
1011 Third Avenue
New York, NY 10021
(866) 939-5267
www.dylanscandybar.com

A wide variety of candies, including seasonal offerings.

ECONOMY CANDY
108 Rivington Street
New York, NY 10002
(800) 352-4544
www.economycandy.com

A good source for old-fashioned and bulk candies, such as black licorice laces.

JELLY BELLY CANDY COMPANY
One Jelly Belly Lane
Fairfield, CA 94533
(800) 522-3267
www.jellybelly.com

The largest selection available of gourmet jelly beans, including bulk sizes of individual flavors. The website offers creative cupcake ideas.

OLD TIME CANDY COMPANY
(866) 929-5477
www.oldtimecandy.com

An interesting selection of nostalgic and novelty candies; large or small quantities can be purchased.

SWEETWORKS
www.sweetworks.net

Small decorative candies like Sixlets.

SUNFLOWER FOOD & SPICE COMPANY
13318 West 99th Street
Lenexa, KS 66215
(913) 599-6448
(800) 377-4693
www.sunflowerfoodcompany.com

A wide variety of colors of candy-coated chocolate-covered sunflower seeds (Sunny Seed Drops).

INDEX

• Hello Cupcake! companion app: look for it at www.hellocupcakeapp.com (available February 2012).

• Follow us on Twitter (@ whatsnewcupcake) to hear what we are saying about cupcakes right now.

• Our Websites: www.hellocupcakebook.com, www.whatsnewcupcake.com Visit our website to see our latest cupcake designs, find information on the newest candies, and get updates on demonstrations, events, and book signings.

Karen Tack and Alan Richardson are the authors of the best-selling *Hello, Cupcake!* and *What's New, Cupcake?*, which have revolutionized cupcake making.

Called the "Cake Whisperer" by *Gourmet* magazine, **Karen Tack** is a cooking teacher and one of the top food stylists in the nation. She has created cupcakes and other desserts for the covers of many of America's top magazines, including *Bon Appétit, Gourmet, Cook's Illustrated, Real Simple, Martha Stewart Living, Good Housekeeping, Ladies' Home Journal, Family Circle, Woman's Day, Every Day with Rachael Ray, Parents, Family Fun, Taste of Home,* and many more. Karen lives with her family in Connecticut.

Alan Richardson is the coauthor of *The Four Seasons of Italian Cooking* and *The Breath of a Wok*, which won the Best International Cookbook Award and the Jane Grigson Award from the International Association of Culinary Professionals (IACP). His work has appeared in dozens of best-selling cookbooks and leading magazines, including *Esquire, GQ, Newsweek,* the *New York Times Magazine, Food & Wine, Saveur, Washington Post Magazine,* and *Gourmet.* Alan lives with his family in New York.